Your New Saltwater Aquarium:

A Step By Step Guide to Creating and Keeping a Stunning Saltwater Aquarium

Guidance from an Aquarium Authority
By Laurren Schmoyer

Copyright © 2014 by Aquatic Experts
Published 2014 by Jmars Ink
All rights reserved.

No part of this publication may be reproduced or transmitted in any form or by any means, mechanical or electronic, including photocopying and recording, or by any information storage and retrieval system, without permission in writing from the publisher.

http://www.aquaticexperts.com
If you have any questions email us at
customerservice@aquaticexperts.com

About the Author

Laurren Schmoyer owned and operated an aquarium store for over 25 years; from its very meager beginnings this store grew into one of the largest aquarium stores on the east Coast. He also owned a service company maintaining freshwater, saltwater and reef aquariums in homes and offices for over 28 years.

He has spent many years teaching and training his customers in the experts' way to keep fish, plants, invertebrates and corals healthy and thriving for years. Laurren's desire and passion is to share his accumulated knowledge, to help everyone become successful aquatic hobbyists. He is the aquarium expert at answers.com as well as creates informative educational products for the pet industry and aquarium hobbyist.

Also on Amazon by Laurren Schmoyer:
The New Reef Aquarium: Setup, Care and Compatibility
Your New Freshwater Aquarium: A Step by Step Guide to Creating and Keeping a Stunning Freshwater Aquarium

This book has been published with the intent to provide accurate and authoritative information in regard to the subject matter within. While every precaution has been taken in preparation of this book, the publisher and author assume no responsibility for errors or omissions. Neither is any liability assumed for damages resulting from the use of the information herein.

Table of Contents

Preface 1
Introduction 2
   Creating a Stunning Saltwater Aquarium 2
Chapter 1 12
   Components to Create a Saltwater Aquarium 12
   THE BIG DECISION! 74
Chapter 2 75
   How to Assemble an Undrilled Aquarium with Live Rock (FOWLR) 75
   14 Steps to Setup Your New Live Rock Aquarium 77
Chapter 3 95
   How to Assemble an Undrilled Aquarium with Artificial Decorations 95
   15 Steps to Setting Up Your Aquarium 97
Chapter 4 111
   How to Assemble a Drilled Aquarium with Live Rock (FOWLR) 111
   Setting Up Your Saltwater Aquarium 112
Chapter 5 149
   How to Assemble a Drilled Aquarium with Artificial Decorations 149
Chapter 6 153
   Water Quality Explained 153
   The Nitrogen Cycle - Aquarium with Live Rock 155
   The Nitrogen Cycle - Aquarium Setup with Artificial Decorations 158
Chapter 7 162
   How to Choose Fish for a Saltwater Aquarium 162
   Bringing Your New Fish Home 201
   Methods to introducing fish to an aquarium: 203

Chapter 8 210

    Invertebrates are Beneficial and Fun 210
    Bringing Your New Invertebrates Home 247
Chapter 9 252
    How and What to Feed Fish and Invertebrates 252
Chapter 10 260
    Setting Up a Saltwater Quarantine Tank 260
    Eight Steps to Setting Up a Quarantine Tank 261
Chapter 11 267
    How to Care for Your Aquarium 267
    15 Steps to Maintaining a Saltwater Aquarium 270
    More Books by the Author on Amazon 280
Appendix 284
    How to Cure Rock Taken From the Ocean 284
Glossary 286
More About the Author 288

Preface

Welcome to the spectacular, colorful, exotic world of saltwater fish keeping! You are taking an exciting plunge, one that will help you build a strong foundation of saltwater knowledge, ensuring yourself a fun and fulfilling future in this magnificent hobby. With the correct equipment and expert fish keeping information, you can create your very own healthy, thriving, striking aquarium.

To help ensure your success, this manual will take you step-by-step through a process to assemble your saltwater aquarium. This guide will help you choose an aquarium, proper filtration system and other necessary equipment needed to succeed. In its pages you will discover and learn expert secrets to maintaining ideal water quality as well as how and what to feed your fish. You will find lists of exciting colorful fish and invertebrates that will live peacefully together along with additional tips and strategies to keep your animals happy and thriving for years.

Introduction

Creating a Stunning Saltwater Aquarium

While setting up a new saltwater aquarium is exciting, it is nothing compared to the experience of adding beautiful living fish treasures to make it stunning. This book has an entire chapter devoted to choosing hardy, colorful fish but let's take a peek at some of the fish that can be kept in your aquarium.

Coral Beauty and African Pygmy Angelfish

Emperor Angelfish (showing adult coloration)

Azure and Yellow Tailed Damsel

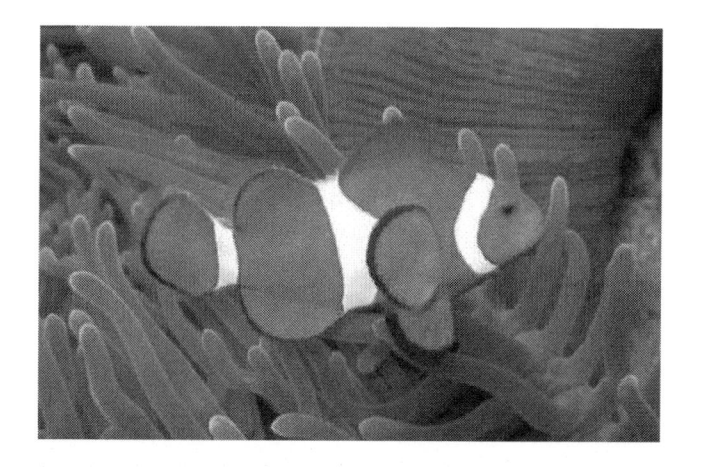

Ocellaris Clownfish made famous by the movie *Finding Nemo*

Royal Gramma and Chalk Bass

Pacific Blue Tang made popular by the movie *Finding Nemo*

Powder Blue and Yellow Tang

Clown Trigger

These are some example of the many gorgeous fish that can thrive in saltwater aquariums. Enjoy the beauty of a fish-only aquarium, or, if you prefer, you can enjoy colorful fish along with zany, playful and entertaining invertebrates, including snails, crabs, urchins, starfish, fan worms, and shrimps. These animals which do not have a backbone are beneficial for saltwater aquariums because they consume unwanted algae, detritus (particles of organic material) and uneaten fish foods. Some invertebrates are simply fun to watch. Let's look at a few that do well in saltwater aquariums.

Blood Red Fire Shrimp

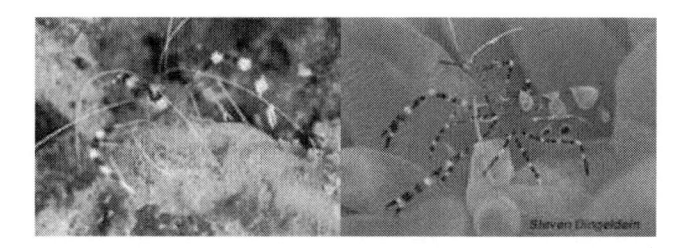

Banded Coral and "Tiny" Spotted Cleaner Shrimp

Skunk Clownfish in Red Carpet Anemone

Coco Worm and close up of a red and white crown

African Red Knob Sea Star

Blue Tuxedo Urchin

As you can see, nature offers an incredibly diverse selection of sea life. You are probably already searching for beautiful fish and cool invertebrates that you would like to have in your aquarium. There is an entire chapter dedicated to invertebrates, filled with information and pictures. As mentioned, many fish and invertebrates can live peacefully together while other fish (triggerfish, for example) may consider them a meal. This book will recommend lots of compatible sea life that will thrive in a home aquarium.

Just because a fish smiles at you is not a good reason to add it to your aquarium

Now let us look at some options to create different scenes inside the aquarium. The current trend is to set up new saltwater aquariums using Fish Only with Live Rock (also known as a FOWLR). Another option is to decorate your aquarium with dead corals or synthetic decorations, which can be removed easily for cleaning. You will need to decide if you prefer the pristine, colorful look of artificial plants and corals, or if you want the natural look of the ocean.

Saltwater aquarium set up with artificial decorations

    The natural look of live rock is the main reason people choose to use it. While it is aesthetically a great move, using natural rock also offers many healthful benefits for the fish. (Live rock is discussed in detail in Chapter 1.) Whichever your budget can afford, both methods offer some of the same benefits.

    Though algae grows on live rock as it does on artificial decorations, algae looks more natural and aesthetically pleasing when growing on live rock as opposed to plastic, silk or resin decorations. Unlike its artificial counterparts, live rock does not need to be removed for cleaning.

    There are also fish and invertebrates that feed on algae; this benefits both the animal and the aquarium and keeps algae under control. Live rock is usually very porous with plenty of surface area to allow beneficial bacteria to colonize and break down waste. The rock can also be stacked to provide hiding places for both fish and invertebrates.

90 gallon bow front aquarium with live rock

90 gallon aquarium with live rock and artificial decorations

One key to success with saltwater aquariums is to keep the inhabitants as relaxed as possible. Whether you choose dead corals and artificial decor or live rock to decorate, you can create a comfortable environment for your fish.

Initially, your aquarium will be pristine and beautiful. Then, as algae grow on the substrate and decor, the aquarium begins to appear dirty. In order to keep your aquarium looking beautiful, the artificial decorations will need to be removed and cleaned. During this process, fish and invertebrates will be disturbed because they use these decorations to define territories. When decorations are put back in the aquarium, territorial struggles begin anew.

Whether you choose artificial decorations or live rock, following this guide will help you enjoy immediate success.

Now it's time to look at the equipment necessary to create your underwater masterpiece.

Chapter 1

Components to Create a Saltwater Aquarium

Let's look at how to choose the right size aquarium for your needs. It is a good rule for a new saltwater fish keeper to purchase the largest aquarium their budget can afford, at least 29 gallons. Many hobbyists end up buying a second aquarium once they find out their first aquarium was too small.

Here are some benefits of a larger aquarium:

- Large aquariums are more stable than their smaller counterparts. Temperature and critical levels in large bodies of water do not fluctuate quickly.
- Large aquariums are more forgiving. If fish are overcrowded or overfed, there is more water to handle the mess.
- You can keep a larger variety of fish and invertebrates in a larger aquarium with many hiding places.
- You can keep large-sized fish.
- You can keep larger numbers of fish and/or schools of small fish.

Once you determine the size you want, you will decide between traditional (undrilled) aquariums and drilled aquariums (ones with holes drilled in the side or bottom). Both are appropriate for setting up saltwater aquariums, therefore we will discuss both types as well as the equipment necessary for each. There are countless filters, pumps and other saltwater components readily available to construct beautiful aquariums. We will also discuss how to choose and stack live rock, as well as the importance of using filtered freshwater not only to mix saltwater, but also to replace evaporated water.

Undrilled Aquariums

90 gallon Traditional/undrilled aquarium (by Aqueon)

Undrilled or standard aquariums cost much less than drilled aquariums and can work well for keeping a saltwater aquarium. The equipment to setup a saltwater aquarium with an undrilled tank costs considerably less than equipment for a drilled one.

Filtration equipment for standard aquariums will be either inside the aquarium or will hang on the side (preferably the back) of the aquarium. The downside is that this equipment is not beautiful and when you look into the aquarium, the equipment will stare back at you.

Another concern is that equipment hanging off the back of the aquarium can quickly become covered in salt or become just plain dusty and dirty. Aquariums are like living pictures, but filtration and other equipment can take away from the overall aesthetics of your creation. A canister filter located in a cabinet below the aquarium can help reduce some of the clutter and will be discussed later.

The best way to keep equipment out of sight is to remove it from the aquarium. There are safe, aesthetically pleasing and effective ways to remove water from an aquarium, filter it, heat it, etc. and return it to the aquarium without flooding the floor. This is done through a single hole or series of holes drilled into the bottom of the aquarium. A drilled aquarium with an overflow box will allow aesthetic advantages, while permitting versatility and the ability to create a beautiful piece of living furniture. Drilled aquariums are wonderful for saltwater because all or most of the unsightly equipment can be installed externally from the aquarium; that way, all that you will see inside the aquarium is an amazing underwater scene.

Drilled Aquariums with Overflows

A drilled aquarium is simply a standard aquarium with holes drilled in the back or bottom. These holes allow water to be removed from and returned to the aquarium. An overflow box is glued into the aquarium to surround the holes.

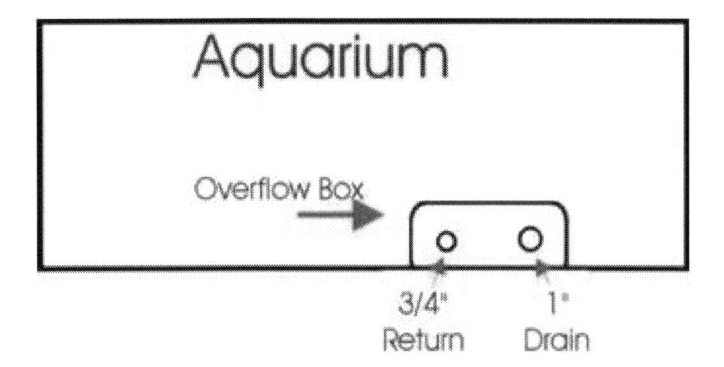

Aquarium
Overflow Box
3/4" Return
1" Drain

This illustration is a top view of two holes drilled in bottom of aquarium with an overflow box surrounding them

Aquarium with overflow box (back view of aquarium)

Overflow boxes are generally made of glass, acrylic, or other food-grade plastic. An overflow box allows the water level in an aquarium to stay full or filled to a desired height. When the water evaporates from an undrilled aquarium, the water level drops in the aquarium. When water evaporates in an aquarium with an overflow box, the water level in the filter drops and the aquarium always stays full. The key is the overflow box is built to a desired height to keep the aquarium full.

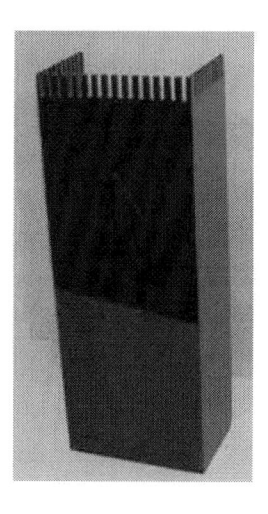

Overflow box with skimming teeth

As long as the water level in the aquarium reaches over the teeth (edge) of the overflow box, surface water will drop into the box, removing floating debris as well as a film that floats on the surface of aquarium water. Removing this film decreases the water's surface tension, allowing gases like carbon dioxide to escape while replenishing life-giving oxygen. This debris-free surface also allows more useable light to penetrate the surface; a plus for photosynthetic corals.

The slimy film removed with the overflow box is actually a combination of proteins, fats, and other organic and non-organic compounds. These compounds, skimmed off the surface of the aquarium water as they drop into the overflow box, travel through tubes through one of the holes drilled in the bottom of the aquarium and into a filter in the cabinet below. This is where the waste is removed.

How it works: A standard overflow box encases two holes drilled into the bottom of an aquarium. Attached to these two holes are two pieces of PVC pipe. The piece with the larger diameter is the drainpipe and the smaller diameter piece is the return. There are many styles of drain piping on the market and aquarists need only ensure that the chosen style is quiet.

Attached to the return pipe is a directional nozzle. This is used to return water back to the aquarium from the filter below.

There are many sizes and shapes of aquariums with overflow boxes already installed. If you already own a traditional aquarium, some fish stores can drill holes in your aquarium and install an overflow box as long as the aquarium glass is not tempered.

> *CAUTION: Tempered glass is often used in aquariums for its strength and because it is relatively lightweight. Before attempting to drill holes in an aquarium, make certain that it DOES NOT have a tempered bottom. If someone tries to drill tempered glass it will shatter like the windshield of a car.*

Next, we need bulkheads, pictured below. The one on the left is used for the return line and the one on the right is for the drain. Each has an O-ring (makes a seal to prevent leaks) and screw-on gasket.

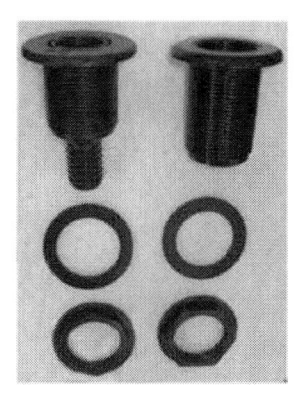

Bulkheads

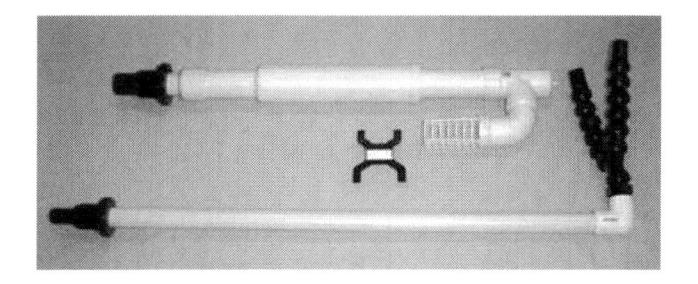

Drain and return assembly with directional nozzle

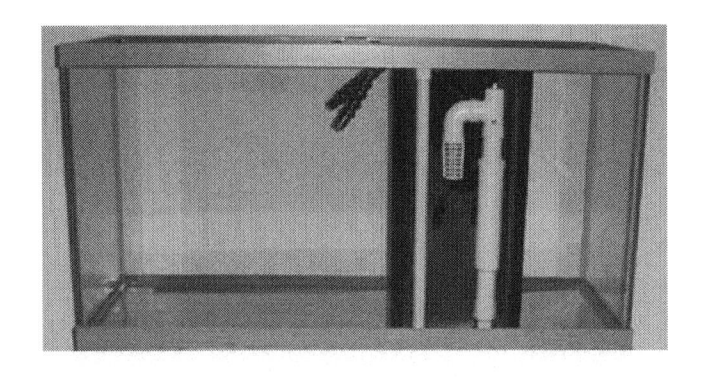

Drain and return assembly installed

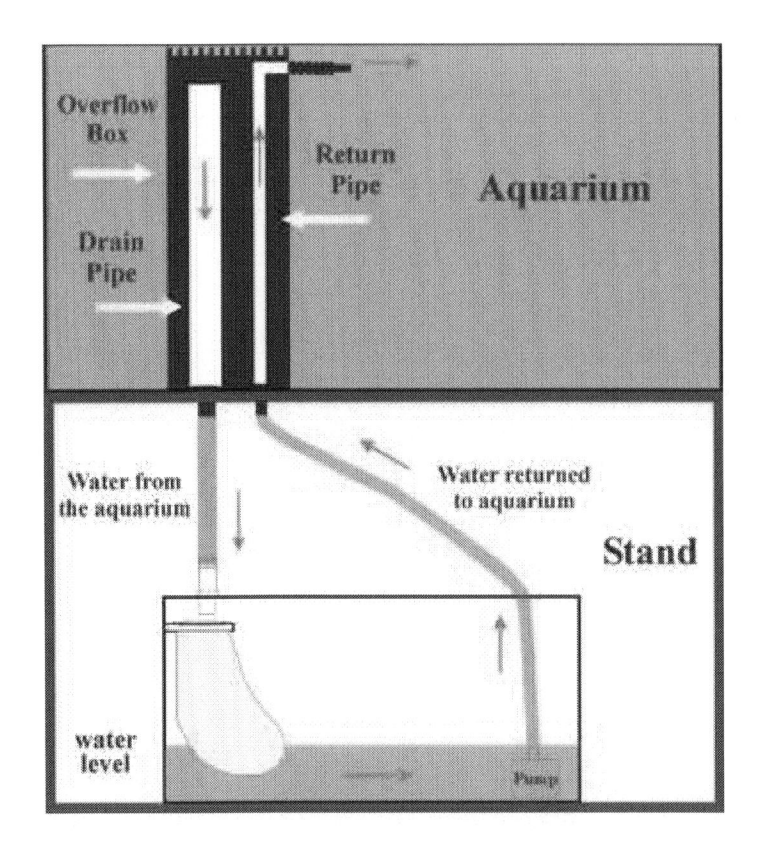

Diagram of a drilled aquarium with simple Berlin filter below in the stand

Choosing a Saltwater Aquarium

When choosing an aquarium, the height, the width, and even the length are very important. Standard aquariums from 20 to 55 gallons are typically 12" from front glass to back glass. When using artificial decoration this narrow width works well since there is a large assortment of sizes available. However stacking live rock in such a space will create an almost vertical rock wall that looks like a cliff. While the wall may appear adequate, wider aquariums (at least 18 inches wide front to back) allow for deep caves, ledges and a more appealing look. Wider tanks offer room to create an open sandy area in front of the rockwork in which fish can swim.

Shallow aquariums (from top to bottom) make for easier cleaning and servicing than their deep counterparts, and also allow more intense light for sea anemones and corals opposed to deep aquariums. That said our best choice is an aquarium 12" to 30" deep.

The length of an aquarium can create the WOW factor. When most people see an aquarium at least 6 feet long in a home, they say "WOW!" Another consideration when choosing a drilled aquarium is to plan for the equipment to be plumbed into a cabinet below it. A larger cabinet makes it easier to house, plumb and service the necessary equipment. Most saltwater hobbyists choose an aquarium three to six feet in length.

Here are a few common saltwater aquarium sizes:
- 65 gallons - 36" (L) x 18" (W) x 24" (H)
- 90 gallons - 48" (L) x 18" (W) x 24" (H)
- 120 gallons - 48" (L) x 24" (W) x 24" (H)
- 180 gallons - 72" (L) x 24" (W) x 24" (H)
- 210 gallons - 72" (L) x 24" (W) x 29" (H)

The shapes of the above aquariums are all rectangular, however you can also create some beautiful saltwater aquariums shaped like cubes, cylinders, bow-fronts - just about any shape you can imagine!

Lighting Explained

Light can reveal beautiful unique colors and patterns of fish and invertebrates; it also dictates whether sea anemones, clams and photosynthetic corals can live in the aquarium.

Light is more than an aesthetic need. Photosynthetic invertebrates like sea anemones and corals contain symbiotic algae (zooxanthellae) living in their tissue which, through photosynthesis, create nutrients for the algae's host. In order for photosynthesis to take place, a specific spectrum of light is required. Our goal is to replicate this light for our photosynthetic invertebrates. If we only plan to keep fish and non-photosynthetic invertebrates such as shrimp, crabs and snails, then a light to optimize their colors is all that is required.

When choosing bulbs (lamps) and light fixtures for your aquarium, it is wise to consider spectrum, intensity as well as lamp types. Since there are so many different sizes, shapes and depths of aquariums, the method to determine the best lighting for your aquarium involves a bit of knowledge and research. In this book we discuss and recommend lighting systems for fish-only and some photosynthetic invertebrates (like sea anemones). For more detailed information on coral lighting, such as intensity, PAR value (Photosynthetically Active Radiation), lighting systems and more, please see the author's book *The New Reef Aquarium: Setup, Care and Compatibility*.

Before we dive into lighting let's look at ways to enclose the top of an aquarium.

Tops, Hoods and Canopies

When you purchase a standard glass or drilled aquarium you have a choice of ways to cover the entire top to keep fish from jumping out, things from falling in and to reduce evaporation. You can purchase a full plastic hood with a light, a glass top or enclosed canopy.

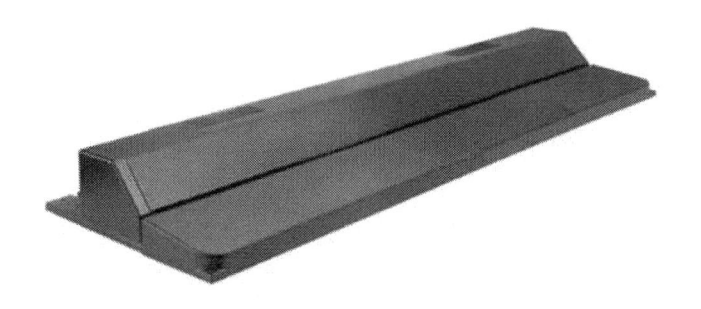

Hood with light fixture for a standard aquarium (by Aqueon)

Aquarium with glass tops and 48" strip light

Wooden Canopy resting on top of aquarium - Front opens for easy access

Canopies with a matching stand can turn an ordinary aquarium into a piece of living furniture. Many pet stores offer custom built stands and canopies to match your home and office decor. Once you decide on an aquarium cover, you can choose light bulbs and a fixture for your aquarium.

Light Fixtures

Typically, aquariums are sold with matching tops and light fixtures. These light fixtures and light bulbs generally work well for fish only aquariums. For smaller aquariums (less than 75 gallons) a single tube strip light is sufficient.

Strip light with one light bulb (by Aqueon)

For more light, most manufactures offer a two bulb fixture. This will make your aquarium and fish look brighter, but more light also can make unwanted algae grow faster.

These standard strip light fixtures house two light bulbs (by Aqueon)

There are many other styles of light fixtures which house two or more bulbs. Some have a protective cover over the bulb so it can be used with or without a glass top.

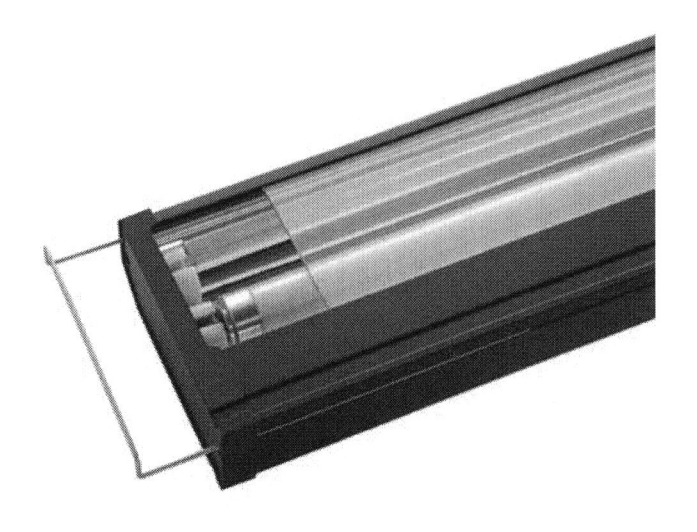

Dual light fixture with protective cover (by Aqueon)

LED Fixtures are also a popular choice. See more information on LED lighting later in this chapter.

LED light fixture (by Marineland)

All of the light fixtures discussed will work well for a fish-only aquarium. Let's look at light bulbs which will bring out the colors in your fish and see what spectrum is needed to grow photosynthetic invertebrates.

Light Bulb Ratings
Most aquarium light bulbs are rated in degrees Kelvin (K), a numerical value attached to color emitted by a light source. A lower value of around 5500 Kelvin is similar to sunlight and gives off a yellow color. A light bulb with a 10000 Kelvin rating (10000K) gives

24

off a crisp white light. Higher Kelvin ratings of 15000 to 20000K light bulbs give off blue to blue violet colors.

There is one particular bulb which radiates blue light, popularly called actinic. A "true" actinic bulb is not sold in degrees of Kelvin; it is manufactured to emit a specific wavelength (420 nm) which is beneficial for corals.

This picture depicts black clips holding two fluorescent bulbs; the top lamp gives off white light and the lower lamp is actinic and gives off blue light

For photosynthetic invertebrates to thrive with good visual colors use a full spectrum of light with extra blue.

Two-lamp fixture with full spectrum and blue light bulb

Most reef aquariums benefit from, and a pleasing color is produced by, 50% blue and 50% white light. Generally light bulbs in standard fixtures will produce a spectrum that enhances the colors in the fish.

Intensity

Choosing lamps that will produce an appealing fish aquarium is easy, but if you are keeping photosynthetic animals in that aquarium we will need to add some power or intensity.

For the most part, the higher the wattage of a light source the deeper the light will penetrate into water. However, different manufacturers have created some products with diverse results. Depending on the lamp, ballast (power source to light the bulbs) and manufacturer we can get different amounts and types of light produced from the same Kelvin-rated bulbs. Because of this, pet and aquarium stores will recommend certain bulbs with certain ballasts to ensure consistent results.

Increasing wattage means more electricity is required to run the light, resulting in higher power bills. One way to reduce this ongoing expense is to use high-polished metal reflectors. Fluorescent lamps give off 360 degrees of light. To make lamps more efficient, use a reflector to direct the majority of that light into your aquarium. Reflectors allow us to use lower wattage lamps to achieve almost the same effect as a lamp with higher wattage.

Light Bulbs Types

Fluorescent and Compact Fluorescent

Typical freshwater or saltwater aquarium setups from pet stores include a fluorescent light fixture with a T8-size light bulb. These bulbs do a good job illuminating a fish-only aquarium but may not provide the intensity necessary to keep photosynthetic animals. Multiple light bulbs can assist in providing intensity, or you can upgrade to more efficient T5 High Output (HO) Fluorescent lamps.

In comparison, T5 fluorescent lamps use less electricity than their T8 predecessors. Also, T5 lamps can produce light almost twice as bright as a standard florescent lamp. Combine a new improved mirror reflector with a T5 bulb and the result is about the same amount of PAR value as the older intense lights with a lower electric bill and less heat.

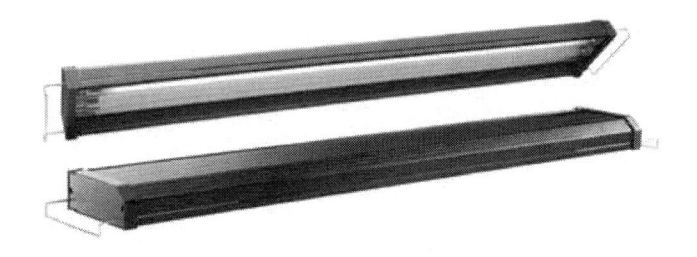

T5 fluorescent lamps with reflectors (by Aqueon)

Another benefit of T5 compared to the old fluorescent lamps is they are physically smaller, only 5/8" in diameter, allowing more light with less space. T5 fluorescent lights work great in aquariums less than 20" deep for keeping low and medium light corals and sea anemones.

When housing photosynthetic corals and other photosynthetic invertebrates, it is best to replace the fluorescent bulbs every year or follow the manufacturer's recommendations.

LED

The newest light to hit the market is LED - and it looks quite promising. Manufacturers claim that LED bulbs provide optimum light output for 50,000 hours! That means you would have over ten years before LED bulbs need to be replaced.

Some high-output LEDs will produce sufficient spectrum and intensity to grow sea anemones and most photosynthetic invertebrates.

LED light fixture by Marineland

LED lights also create a shimmering effect with low power consumption. In addition, LEDs, unlike many lights, radiate heat away from the water. LED aquarium fixtures usually include white and blue bulbs.

LED white and blue bulbs with reflector around each bulb

Some fixtures have dimmers to allow customization of the color to personal preference. Some people like a whiter looking aquariums, while others prefer a bluish tint to the water. Dimming the LEDs also allows you to create different light phases; daylight, sunrise to sunset, and simulate cloud movement and moon phases.

At this time LED lighting fixtures are uniquely made by each manufacturer. It is best to choose a trusted manufacturer and go with their recommendations.

Moonlight LEDs

To view an aquarium at night without disturbing its inhabitants, place a light fixture over the aquarium with one or several blue LEDs. After the main aquarium lights go off at night, these few blue LEDs generate a beautiful blue shimmering light, adding a calming and even majestic ambiance.

36" LED fixture with two moonlight bulbs

These blue LEDs, when turned on at nighttime, are called moonlights and they provide enough light to watch any activity, make some corals fluoresce and create a stunning effect.

If you plan to use a drilled aquarium you may skip the next section and go to "Filtration for Drilled Aquariums"

Filtration for undrilled Aquariums

Fish waste and uneaten fish food break down into several compounds, one of which is ammonia. High levels of ammonia are toxic to fish and invertebrates. Biological filtration reduces ammonia to nitrite, then to a final product called nitrate. Natural seawater is continuously moving; reef areas, where high levels of nitrates are produced, are constantly being replenished with low-nitrate water from the ocean depths. In a closed system like an aquarium, levels of ammonia, nitrite and nitrate can quickly rise to toxic levels. This is why it is necessary to filter aquarium water.

Hang-on Filters

Most novice hobbyists purchase hang-on filters not only because they are inexpensive, but also because the majority of the ones on the market today will work in both salt and freshwater. A power filter hangs on the back of the aquarium and a small pump pulls water up through an intake (siphon) tube and into the filter. The water is then directed through filter media and spills back into the aquarium.

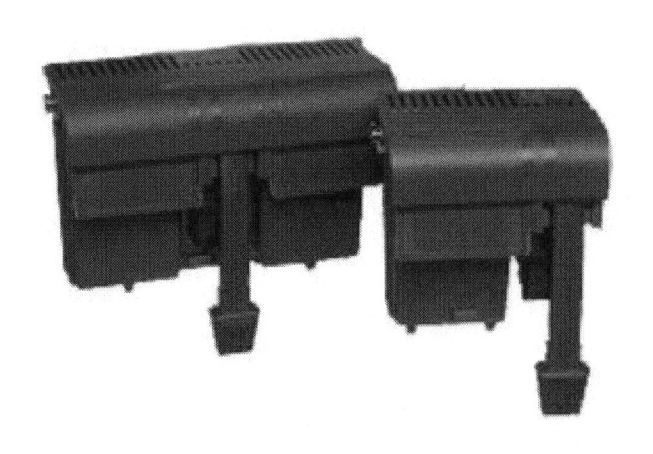

Two popular hang-on-filters

The size of the aquarium dictates what size power filter to use and filters generally have flow rates written on their boxes. A power filter should have a flow rate of 6 to 8 times the number of gallons of the aquarium; if you have a 55-gallon aquarium, you need a filter that pumps from 330 - 440 gallons per hour.

It is critical when the water from the power filter is returned to the aquarium, it ripples the surface of the water. The top 1/16" of the surface is where gas exchange takes place, to oxygenate the water and release CO_2 there needs to be surface movement (unless oxygenation takes place in the filter).

Filter cartridges, sponge and bio-wheel

Mechanical filters are made of a floss cartridge, pad or sponge. Mechanical media traps large particulate matter such as excess food that may be floating around in the water. The biological portion of a filter is made of ceramic rings, plastic bio balls, sponges, or fiber wheel(s). This biological media serves as surface area on which helpful bacteria break down fish waste and other organic nutrients can grow. Chemical filtration is generally achieved through a high-quality grade of activated filter carbon. Carbon adsorbs dissolved organics, which reduces odors and removes yellow color from the water.

TIP: When using live rock in your aquarium the rock becomes your biological media, making other biological media unnecessary in the filter.

Power filters are easy to maintain. The key is that they require regular maintenance. Since each filter is different, refer to the manufacturers' instructions. General maintenance for filters with cartridges is to rinse cartridges every week to removed debris and replace them each month. To keep a filter's optimum flow rate, make sure you clean the inside of the siphon tube with a test tube brush. It may also become necessary to remove the impeller and clean it.

Canister filters

Canister filters come in a variety of different sizes and are sold according to their flow rates. A canister filter generally sits below an aquarium, allowing the aquarium to sit closer to a wall. (Hang-on filters space the aquarium and stand several inches away from the wall.) Canisters are also designed to hold more filter media than hang-on filters.

Canister filters can be square or cylindrical in shape. They come with two flexible tubes attached to the lid of the filter. One tube takes water from the aquarium, the other channels water from the filter back into the aquarium.

Canister filter with large chambers

Each manufacturer makes its canister filter a little differently, but they all work basically the same. Once the water enters the filter, it is channeled through a series of trays or containers that hold various types of filter media. The water usually passes through some type of mechanical media, comprised of a foam or fiber pad to remove large particles. Next, it flows through a chamber filled with a chemical media such as activated filter carbon or a resin to remove dissolved organic compounds and chemicals from the water. Other chambers can be filled with bio media (ceramic rings, plastic bio balls, etc.), or other media of your choice. It is important to note that when using live rock with a good flow of water, the rock works as the biological media, and no additional bio media is needed.

Once water has been cycled through the filter, the newly clean water is pumped back to the aquarium through tubes and is forced either through a spray bar or through a return with a deflector. A spray bar is a long bar with a series of holes drilled in a straight line the length of the bar. When water is forced through all these holes causing a "spray" action, a large section of the surface water is moved. Some filters use a deflector to force the return water in a particular direction. Some deflectors can rotate allowing the top of the water to ripple in various directions.

Canister filters are extremely quiet. They take slightly more time to clean than hang-on filters.

Some benefits of canister filters:
- The aquarium and stand can be placed closer to the wall.
- They can hold large amounts and different types of filter media.
- They are very quiet when running.
- A UV sterilizer can be easily plumbed in-line with a canister filter.

NOTE: Water density and temperature have a direct effect on oxygen levels in a saltwater aquarium. Since saltwater is denser than freshwater, it holds less oxygen. Another determining factor for oxygen content in an aquarium is water temperature. The higher the temperature the less oxygen is found in the water. To keep oxygen levels at optimum levels it is crucial to make sure you have the right size filter and it is working at 100%.

Adding an Ultra Violet Sterilizer

An in-line ultra violet sterilizer can be readily added when using a canister filter. Simply cut the flexible tubing that returns water to the aquarium. Attach one end of the tubing to one side of the UV and the other cut end to the other side of the sterilizer. Use clamps on the tubing to ensure a tight seal.

Filtration for Drilled Aquariums

There are two styles of filters used with drilled aquariums: wet/dry or Berlin. Wet/dry filter is used for aquariums with fish, invertebrates and artificial decorations while a Berlin filter is used for aquariums with fish, invertebrates and live rock.

Wet/Dry or Trickle Filters

A wet/dry filter, or trickle filter, is a biological and mechanical filter encased within a sump to store excess water (see glossary for more details). This filter is designed to be used with tanks containing no other biological filter media.

Acrylic wet/dry or trickle filter

Wet/dry filters provide the surface area necessary for beneficial bacterial growth. These filters are typically used in fish-only systems. These filters are generally located below the aquarium.

Water from the aquarium is routed through the overflow box down to a filter. A wet/dry filter can be constructed out of glass or plastic.

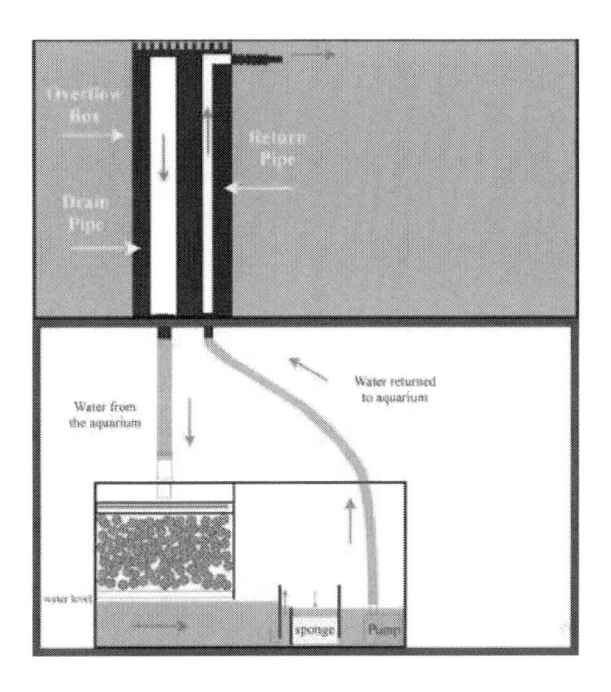

Diagram shows placement of wet/dry filter and water flow

There are many different designs of wet/dry filters but they all basically work in the same manner. Water drains through a vacuum tube as shown below. This tubing is attached directly to a pipe at the top of the wet/dry filter.

Drain tube (vacuum tube) is the gray tube on left and the black return tube is on the right; both are attached to bulkhead fittings in the overflow

    This water is poured or sprayed into the top compartment of the filter. There is usually a tray or area for filter media to remove the larger particles from your water.
    Once the water passes through the (mechanical) filter media it falls onto a tray with holes. These holes help spread the water out evenly allowing for a shower effect below. The water then drops onto the filter media.

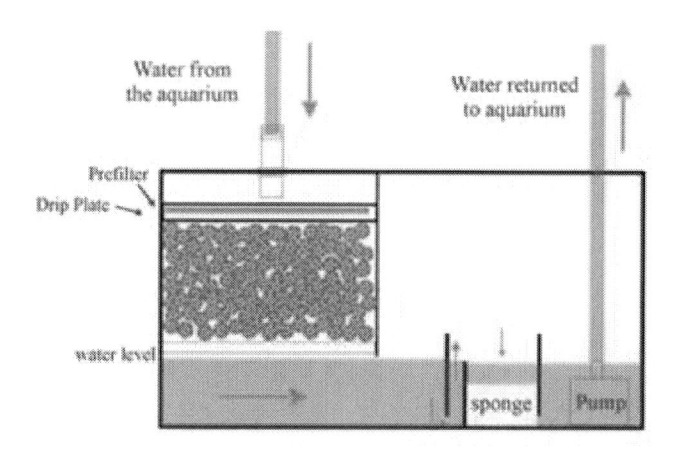

Example of a wet/dry filter

Wet/dry filters contain plastic biological media (bio-media), the blue balls pictured below. Commonly available bio-media come in a variety of shapes and sizes and are most often seen shaped like balls or plastic strips. This ball-shaped media normally has ridges, projections and holes in order to provide more surface area for bacterial growth.

Attaching vacuum hose to wet/dry filter

As the water flows through the bio-media it comes in contact with beneficial nitrifying bacteria that live on the surface of the media. These bacteria break down fish waste and other organic compounds making the aquarium non-toxic and safe for fish. (See "Nitrogen Cycle" in the glossary for more details.)

Bio-media is kept out of the water that collects in the bottom of the filter by a grate. A stream of water from the aquarium above flows over the bio-balls. Keeping the bio media chamber above the water level in the filter provides an environment high in oxygen, which is extremely beneficial to nitrifying bacteria, enabling the filter to be more efficient in removing biological wastes.

NOTE: New filter media does not have any bacteria. If cycling naturally, it takes approximately 4 to 6 weeks to have sufficient bacterial growth to effectively process fish waste. Always test your system for ammonia and nitrites before adding additional livestock.

Another benefit of the bio-media in a wet/dry filter is that the large total surface area allows the water flowing through it to spread into a very thin layer. This allows for efficient exchange of gases, aiding in oxygenation of the aquarium water. The higher dissolved oxygen level ensures a healthy environment for aquarium inhabitants.

TIP: The flow rate of water through the wet/dry filter needs to be slow enough that the water has time to contact the plastic media. Water passing through the wet/dry should be turned over at a rate of approximately 4 to 6 times per hour, meaning a 100 gallon aquarium should have 400 to 600 gallons of water passing through the wet/dry filter per hour. The typical fish-only tank should have a total turnover of 6 to 8 times per hour, with the difference being made up by powerheads, discussed soon.

Below the media is the sump where water is stored. This water is used to keep the aquarium full. If the water level in the aquarium drops below the teeth on the overflow box water will no longer travel to your filter. Water naturally evaporates from the aquarium and sump; therefore it is important to choose a sump that can hold a large volume of water in anticipation of evaporation.

Another benefit of a large size sump is that it allows room for a heater, protein skimmer and internal pump. Most wet/dry filters also have compartments where chemical adsorption media like carbon can be placed.

The final piece of a wet/dry filter is an internal pump placed inside the sump or an external pump attached to the outside of the sump to return cleaned water to the aquarium.

TIP: A piece of Styrofoam placed under a wet/dry filter will allow the filter to level itself and remove any unevenness from the stand.

Berlin Filters

A Berlin filter has a sump or water holding chamber with a mechanical filter and space for a protein skimmer and other equipment. It is usually placed below the aquarium and preferably in a cabinet stand. Berlin filter can be very basic or may be extremely deluxe with lots of compartments and built in refugium walls.

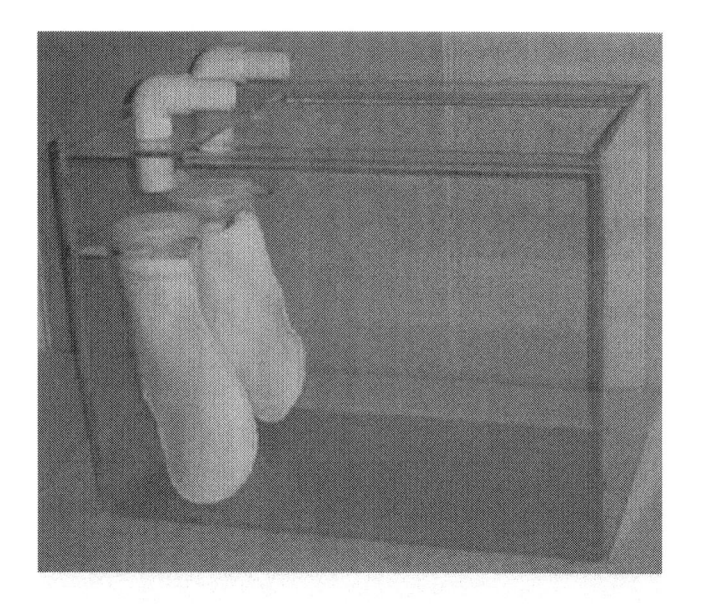

Basic - Berlin sump with two sock hangers and filter socks

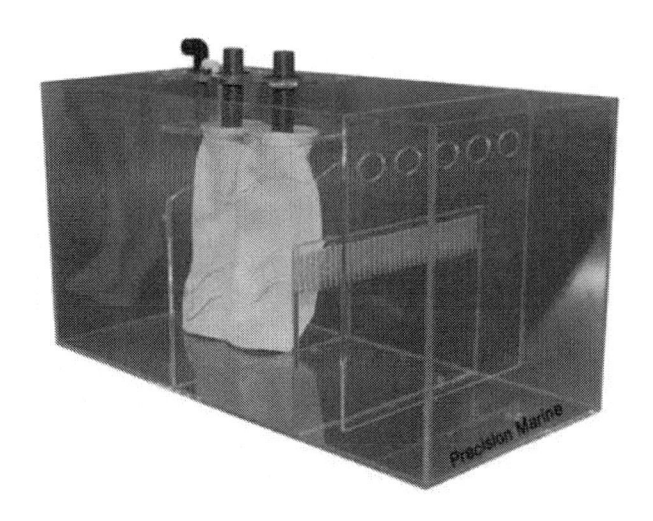

Deluxe - sump has two sock hangers, refugium compartment, protein skimmer and return water pump compartment

A Berlin filter is placed below the aquarium, usually in a cabinet stand. Water is routed from the overflow box of the aquarium through a drain line down to the Berlin filter. This water then flows through a pre-filter and collects in the bottom of the filter.

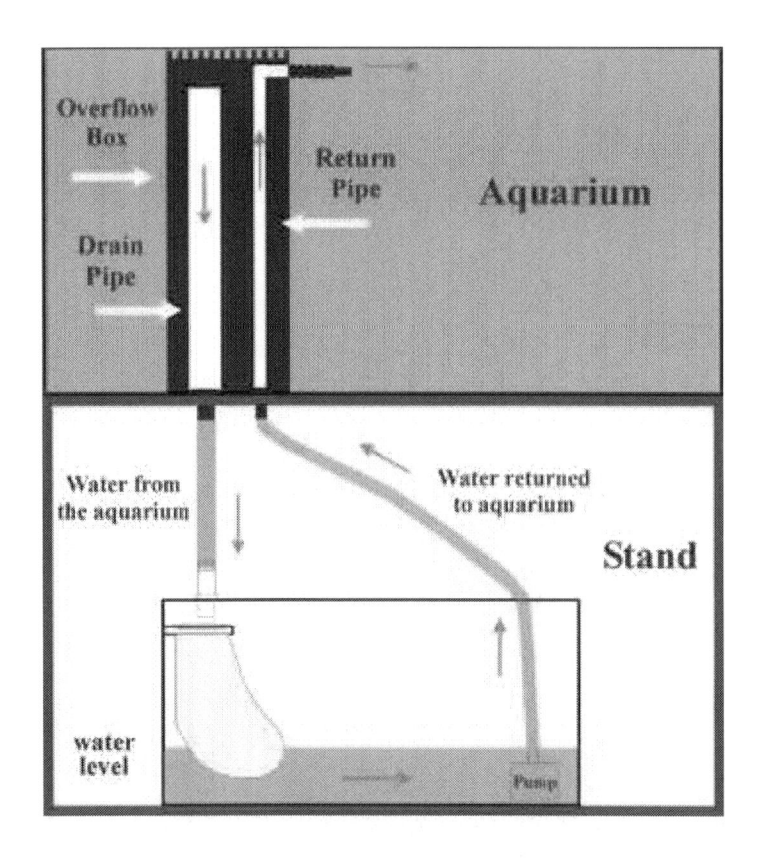

Diagram shows placement of Berlin filter and water flow

    The pre-filter can be a sheet of fiber material in a tray or a filter bag or sock, as pictured. The purpose of the pre-filter is to physically or mechanically remove large particles from the water. The sock(s) and other pre-filter materials should be cleaned and/or replaced often. The amount of livestock will dictate how often the media must be cleaned or changed.

    As a filter sock gets dirty, the water inside the sock rises until it eventually flows over the top of the sock. All physical filtration media will eventually clog with debris and must be replaced. The more often you clean your media, the better the water quality of your aquarium. A dirty mechanical filter will eventually lead to increased nitrates as bacteria grow in the media to process the accumulated waste. Hence, it is important to replace physical filtration media often.

After solid debris is removed from aquarium water by the pre-filter, the water can be processed through a protein skimmer, one of the main keys to filtration in a Berlin system.

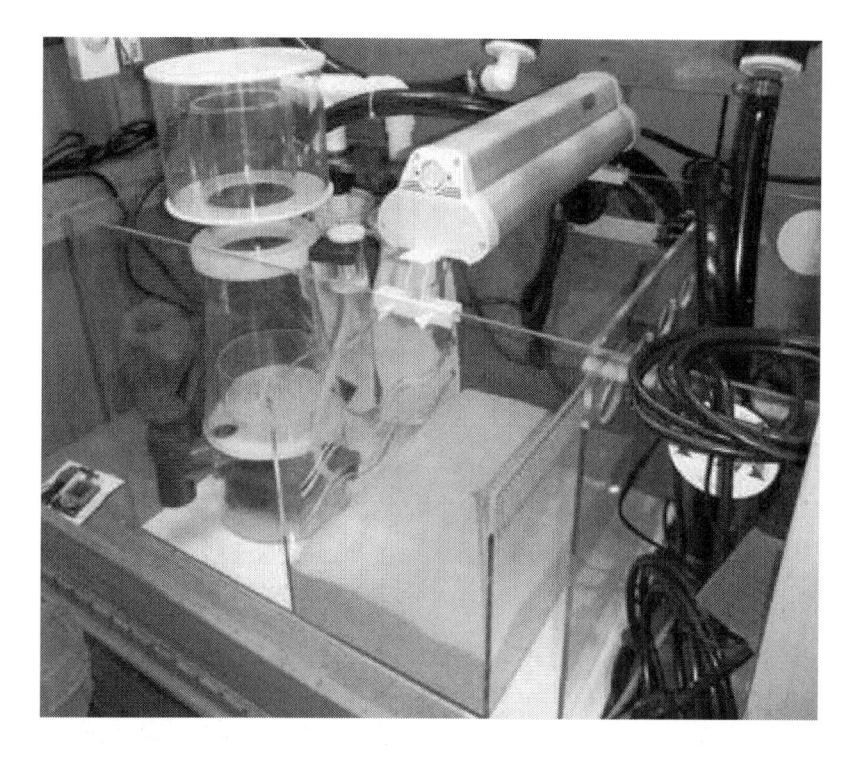

Berlin filter, protein skimmer and refugium compartment in center with white sand

The Berlin filter also holds the return pump and heater, which allows the display tank to be free of the clutter of necessary aquarium equipment.

Protein Skimmers

Have you ever noticed the foam left when waves crash on the shore as you stroll along the beach?

Waves crashing on the beach leave protein foam and other wastes behind

This foam is composed of protein and wastes from the ocean. Protein skimmers attempt to mimic the action caused by these aerated, crashing waves.

Protein skimmers physically remove dissolved organic compounds and other substances from aquarium water. These organic compounds are a product of uneaten fish foods, fish waste, dead plants, bacteria and decomposing matter. Organic compounds in the water break down into several by-products, one of which is ammonia.

High levels of ammonia are toxic to fish and invertebrates. Biological filtration reduces ammonia to a final product called nitrates. Natural seawater is continuously moving, and reef areas where high levels of nitrates are produced are constantly being replenished with low-nitrate water from the ocean depths. In a closed system like an aquarium levels of nitrate can quickly rise to toxic levels.

Protein skimmers remove wastes before they are broken down into nitrates. That means higher water quality for aquarium inhabitants.

Example of internal protein skimmer

Internal protein skimmer in Berlin sump

How Does A Skimmer Work?

There are many types and designs of protein skimmers. Most skimmers have some basic components in common. They consist of a vertical chamber filled by a pump where water is mixed with fine bubbles. Dissolved organic compounds are attracted to the surface of the bubbles within the skimmer and join themselves to the bubbles as they rise.

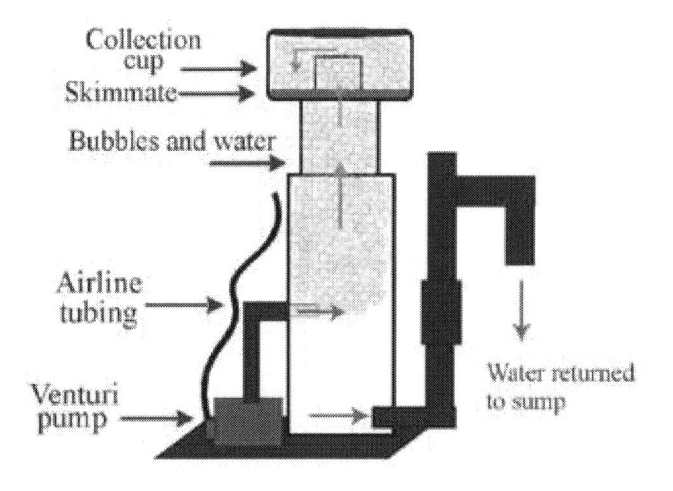

In-sump protein skimmer - Water is pumped from the sump into a column of water and bubbles then returns to the sump

As these bubbles rise to the top of the chamber they produce foam. This foam is the same foam you see washed up on shore at the beach. As the foam rises up the chamber it falls into a collection cup. The bubbles pop and the compounds are collected in a cup and removed from the aquarium water. The product that is collected in the cup is referred to as skimmate. The collection cup is emptied periodically to remove these wastes from the system.

There are four general configurations of protein skimmers: internal protein, hang-on aquarium, in-sump and freestanding skimmers. In each of these categories, you will find many designs.

> *TIP: A skimmer that is too small will not operate effectively and will require more maintenance than one that is sized correctly for the gallons in the reef. Skimmer sizing on retail packaging can be rather general, and it may be prudent to purchase a skimmer that is rated for a larger aquarium.*

Choosing a Quality Protein Skimmer

Here is what you need to know when choosing a protein skimmer.

The size of the bubble is very important. If the bubble is large, it will rise to the surface quickly. Smaller bubbles rise more slowly in the water column than larger bubbles, giving more time for organic compounds to attach to them. Small bubbles also have more surface area than large bubbles (in the same size skimmer) providing more surface area to which organic compounds can attach.

The water column in your protein skimmer should be almost white with bubbles. This means there will be millions of bubbles in the water column. If there is a lot of water with just a few bubbles, the skimmer will not efficiently remove organic compounds.

An efficient protein skimmer will have thick, dark-colored waste in its collection cup. If the waste is watery and pale greenish or yellow in color adjust the water level or bubble size.

The waste collection cup should be easy to remove for cleaning.

This protein skimmer sits inside a Berlin sump; note the white column of fine bubbles

Protein skimmers require periodic cleaning to keep them running efficiently. When choosing a protein skimmer, be sure the parts that need cleaning are easily accessible and removable.

Water Pumps and Powerheads

Water Pumps
Overflow boxes skim water off the surface of an aquarium and channel water down to a wet/dry or Berlin filter. A pump then returns the water to your aquarium.

The pump can be internal (placed inside the Berlin filter) or external (outside the Berlin filter). Choose a pump designed to handle saltwater.

Internal Water Pumps

Internal water pumps come in an assortment of sizes based on how many gallons per hour it pumps. It generally cost less than external pumps.

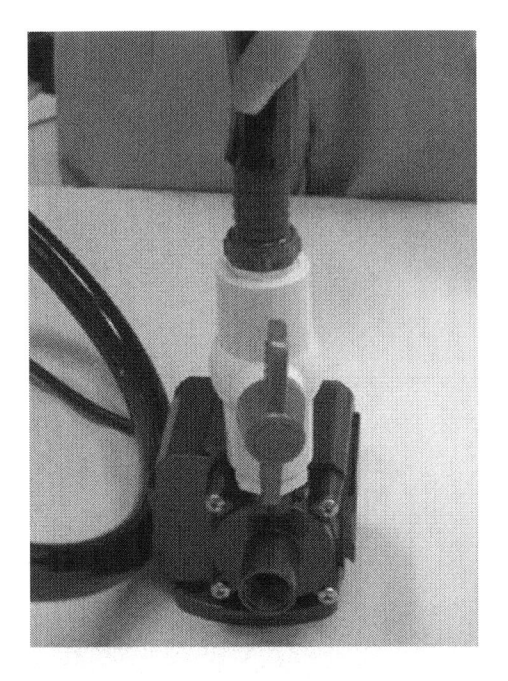

Internal pump

Advantages of Internal Water Pumps
- Easy to install and replace.
- If the pump or fittings to the pump ever leak water drains back into the filter.
- Pumps are usually very quiet.
- Generally compact in size.

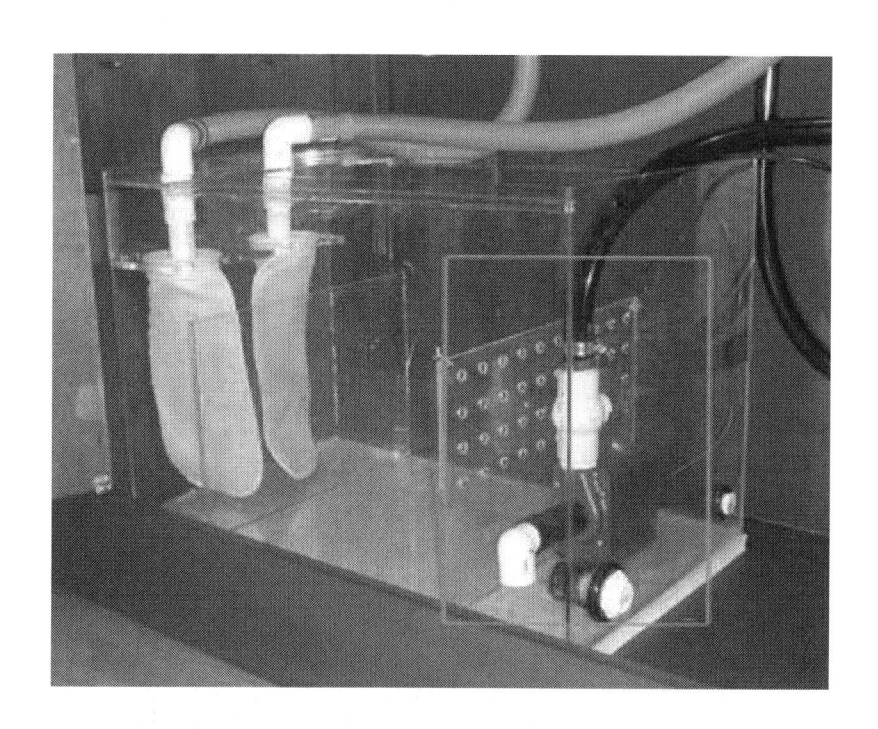

Internal water pump in sump on right

External Water Pumps

Most external water pumps have a cooling fan built in to remove the heat the pump generates. This means less heat is transferred directly to the aquarium water. These water pumps come in an assortment of sizes based on how many gallons per hour it pumps. External water pumps need a hole cut into the filter with piping to channel the water outside the filter to the pump.

External water pump

Advantages of External Water Pumps
- Available in larger sizes for big aquariums.
- Leaves room inside the Berlin filter for other equipment.
- Very little heat is transferred to the aquarium water.
- Noisy water pumps can be plumbed at a location away from the aquarium.

External pump plumbed into a Berlin filter

Choosing the Right Size Water Pump

Ideally, you want to turn your aquarium water over between three to five times each hour through your sump. Therefore, if you have a 90-gallon aquarium you need to have a pump that can pump 270 to 450 gallons each hour.

Another important factor in selecting a pump is "head pressure". Head pressure is determined by how high the pump is returning water to your aquarium. If the water pump is located under your aquarium and it has to push water back over the side of the aquarium we would measure that the height (in feet) of the side of the aquarium to determine the head pressure.

If we measure the height from the pump to the aquarium rim and it is at four feet than we have four feet of head pressure.

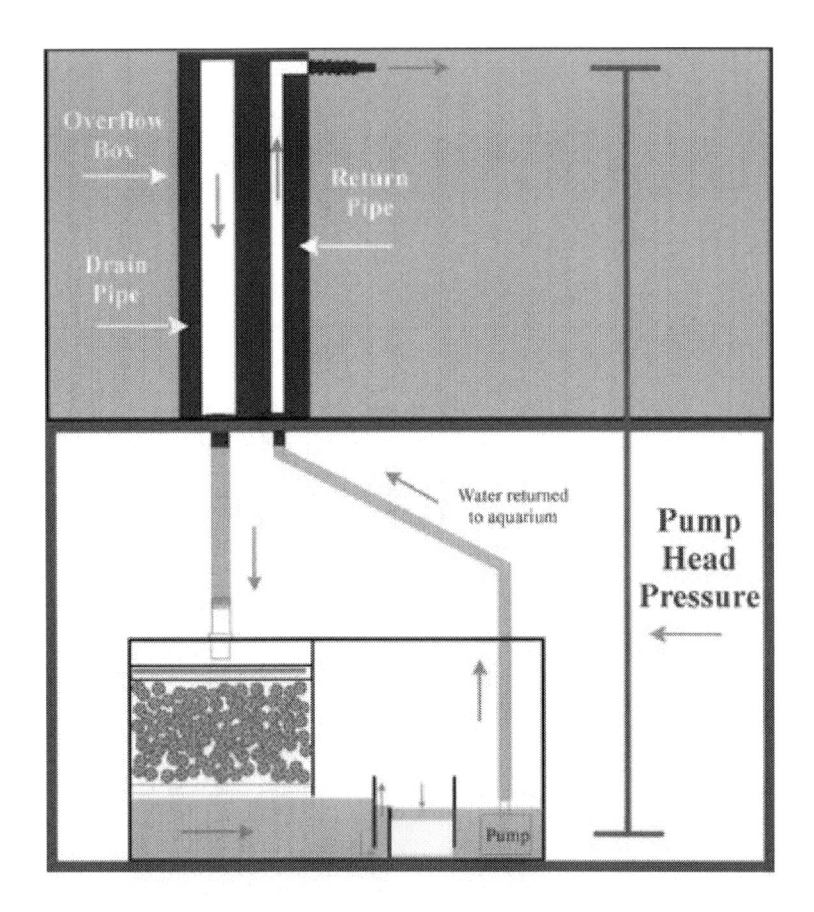

Diagram shows the head pressure from the pump to the return pipe

Each water pump manufacturer has a chart showing the number of gallons the pump pushes at different head pressures. Once you determine the amount of water (in gallons) you want your aquarium to turn over in a given hour use the chart to choose the correct size pump for your aquarium.

Powerheads

A powerhead is a small submersible water pump. They have many uses including:
- Circulation of water inside your aquarium.
- Pumping water through protein skimmers, UV sterilizers, reactors and other equipment.

Powerheads are ideal for additional circulation inside your aquarium. Many times there are areas of low flow within an aquarium. Mounting a small powerhead with its nozzle pointing in the direction where extra flow is needed will ensure you have water movement throughout your aquarium.

Examples of powerheads

Just like water pumps, powerheads are rated by the number of gallons per hour of water they pump. It is important that the flow rate of the powerhead is suitable to the particular application for which it is intended. Check the chart that comes with the particular brand and model you want to use.

Powerheads are available in a nozzle or wide flow style. Powerheads with a nozzle output (which produce a straight, or linear, high pressure flow) are easy to attach to tubing used in conjunction with protein skimmers, UV sterilizers, and other equipment. They are also useful in situations where the aquarist needs flow directed in a specific area in the aquarium.

Powerheads with a wide flow output (called diffuse flow) are useful in creating general flow throughout the aquarium. These powerheads are commonly used in tanks with live rock to ensure flow throughout the water column in the tank. These pumps also move a high water volume at a low pressure, creating a wide, gentle flow when compared to the constricted jet of water created by nozzle-output powerheads. This wider flow at low pressure is especially essential in reef tanks, assuring filter feeding invertebrates have access to suspended food particles in the aquarium water.

When used within an aquarium, a powerhead can be attached with a hanger, suction cups, or magnets. Over time suction cups stiffen and lose their grip on the aquarium glass. The hanger style limits where you can place your powerhead in your aquarium to an area within several inches of the tank's rim. The best choice is a magnetic clip-on style. Magnets make for easy placement anywhere on the glass of your aquarium and won't give out over time.

Wavemaker

Wavemakers create random current throughout the aquarium. Most aquariums have spots of no or low water flow areas around corals or live rock where waste accumulates. A wave like action and random currents will send the waste up into the water column where it can be removed by mechanical filtration.

There are many different types and styles of wavemakers, but we will focus on the ones which control multiple water pumps and powerheads. Normally water pumps and powerheads create a constant stream of water. Once their power cords are plugged into a wavemaker they can now create random currents. The wave maker can turn water pumps or powerheads on and off and some can even increase or decrease the flow rate. Wavemakers can range from inexpensive to very expensive.

Example of a wavemaker controller

The low end models are basically timers that turn your powerheads on and off every 15 to 90 seconds. The more expensive models have buttons you push to change the different types of wave patterns. Some will include a button to push for feeding that turns the powerheads off or down and leaves the main water pump running. This period of time allows the fish to eat without its food being blown around the aquarium. Some have night cycles which reduce the water currents.

Refugium

Because of its many benefits to a saltwater or reef aquarium a refugium makes a great addition. Like inlets and saltwater marshes, modern refugiums house microorganisms and macro algae nestled on a deep sand and/or mud bed with live rock. A refugium can be as simple as a glass aquarium or an acrylic box with chambers created by partitions or baffles, with a light placed above it.

Refugiums provide many benefits to the main or display aquarium. Macro algae, mud and/or sand become natural filters for reducing nitrates, silicates, and phosphates. Reducing excess organic nutrients helps control unwanted algae growth in the display aquarium. Also, the refugium lights are set to turn on at times opposite the display aquarium, stabilizing oxygen and pH levels.

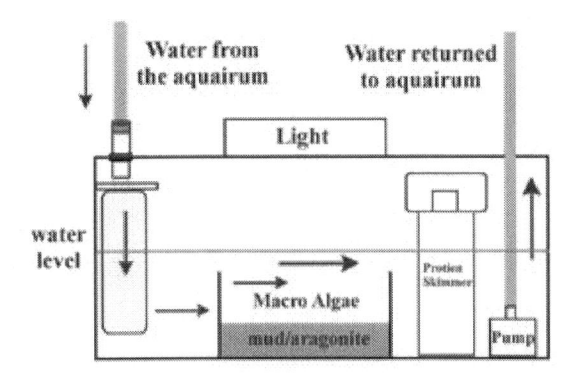

Pictured is a refugium with deep substrate and thick plant life

Since the refugium is generally separate from the main aquarium, it provides protection for copepods and amphipods (sold at most aquarium stores) giving your aquarium a constant, natural food source. This natural food can be netted from the refugium or will travel naturally to the display aquarium via the lines connecting the two. To keep this natural food source, never put predators such as fish, shrimp, and corals in your refugium.

Refugium Styles

Refugiums come in a variety of styles including hang-on, internal, stand-alone and built-in.

A **hang-on refugium** consists of an acrylic box with baffles, a small, submersible water pump to pump water from the aquarium into the refugium, and a light. The water flows through the refugium and gravity feeds it back to the aquarium. Just add mud or sand and macro algae and it is ready to go.

An **internal refugium** is built inside the main aquarium with sections of the aquarium divided off.

A **stand-alone refugium** is housed in an aquarium outside the display aquarium. This style refugium uses an aquarium with dividers or baffles, a pump and a return system. The stand-alone refugium can be attached above, beside or below your display aquarium. Depending on the location of the refugium the water is either pumped or gravity fed back to the main aquarium.

A **built-in refugium** is built into a trickle filter or Berlin sump. Water is normally gravity fed from the main aquarium through pre-filtered media (to remove large debris) then through the refugium. A series of glass or acrylic walls allow water to pass through the refugium section, keeping mud and algae from passing through the return-line to the display aquarium. These walls also slow water flow to assist with macro algae feeding.

Built-in-refugium with sand, macro algae and light

The size refugium needed, depends on the bio-load of the display aquarium. A larger refugium is necessary for a heavily stocked display aquarium; a smaller refugium may be used for a lightly stocked aquarium.

Once a refugium style is chosen and it is plumbed to the display aquarium and is ready to set up. Add a commercial refugium mud and/or an oolithic (sugar size) aragonite sand to a depth of up to six inches; add live rock and macro algae.

Macro Algae

Chaetomorpha, Ulva (Sea Lettuce), halimeda (red seaweed) and Gracilaria (red seaweed) are macro algae that do well in refugiums. These macro algae remove nitrates and phosphates from aquarium water. Regular trimming and thinning of these plants also removes phosphates and nitrates from the system.

Lighting

Place a light over the refugium to grow macro algae. The bulb should be 5,000 to 6,500 Kelvin for optimum plant growth. Choose a light fixture that produces at least 4 watts per gallon of water in the refugium (for those less than 16 inches deep).

TIP: Use an appliance timer and set the refugium light to turn on when the display light goes out.

During the day, when exposed to light, plants and algae in the display aquarium use up carbon dioxide and give off oxygen. When the display aquarium light is off photosynthesis no longer takes place and CO2 levels rise. Carbon dioxide (CO2) is an acid, so pH lowers at night when the light is out.

With a refugium light on while the display aquarium lights are off, plants in the refugium will use CO2 and produce oxygen keeping the pH in the entire system stable. This ensures the nighttime oxygen levels do not drop as sharply as in a reef without a refugium.

Ultra Violet Sterilizers

A UV Sterilizer (UV for short) uses an ultraviolet light to kill single-celled organisms such as bacteria, viruses, protozoan, and algae cells that are floating in water which passes past the UV bulb.

A UV consists of a plastic or stainless steel housing through which water is pumped around and past a germicidal bulb. It is best to use a UV that uses a quartz sleeve between the bulb and the water. The quartz sleeve makes it easier to change the bulb.

These units come in two styles: Hang-on or in-line. Water is pumped through the sterilizer using a powerhead, a canister filter, or an internal or external water pump.

Ultraviolet light has a wavelength between 250 and 280 nm which kills organisms by altering their DNA at the cellular level. UV units are effective in eliminating most disease-causing organisms and when used properly, go a long way towards keeping a healthy aquarium.

There are several factors that influence the efficiency of a UV sterilizer:

- Contact time between water and UV bulb (dwell time)
- Clarity of water
- Age of bulb
- Intensity or wattage of bulb

The contact time between the water and the bulb is critical - if the water's flow rate is too fast, contact time with the UV light is reduced so that the sterilizer is ineffective. The flow rate should be slow enough to maximize the time water spends within the UV's housing (check manufacturer's recommended flow rate for your particular model).

The clarity of the water being sterilized is another factor influencing the efficiency of the unit. Ultraviolet sterilizers are typically placed in-line after water leaves the filter for this reason. The cleaner the water, the more efficient the sterilizer will be.

The age of the UV bulb directly relates to the effectiveness of a UV sterilizer. The sterilization impact of the UV drops considerably after about six months to one year of use (depending on the unit). The bulb will still light up, but the spectrum of the lamp will have shifted and it is no longer as effective at killing free-floating organisms.

UV sterilizers are designed to hang on the back of an aquarium or plumbed-in-line between your filter's return pump and your aquarium. This ensures that 100 percent of the water that passes through the sump also goes through the UV. Make sure the UV sterilizer and the return pump are the proper size for your aquarium.

40 watt inline UV sterilizer

Another way to plumb an inline UV sterilizer into your aquarium is to drop a smaller water pump into your sump and push the water through the sterilizer and return it back to the sump. This is easy to install but does not allow for 100 percent of the water to pass through the sterilizer. Again to be most effective have all the water returning to the aquarium pass through the correct size UV sterilizer.

CAUTION: Never look at a UV bulb while it is on. UV light will severely damage the retina. The UV bulb is shielded inside of housing for your protection.

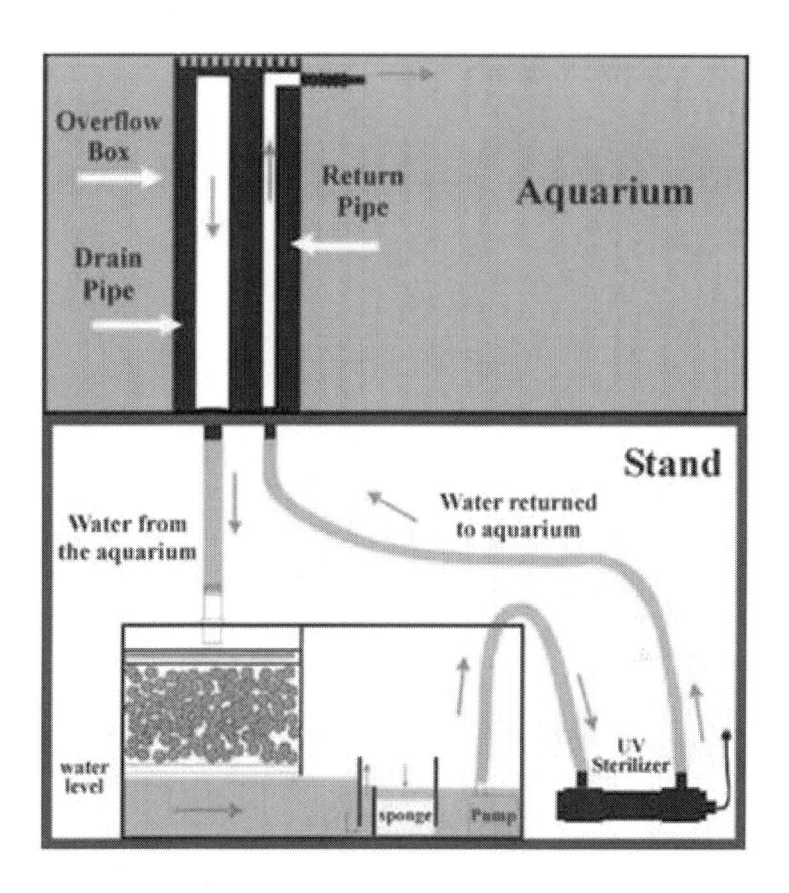

Diagram of inline UV sterilizer

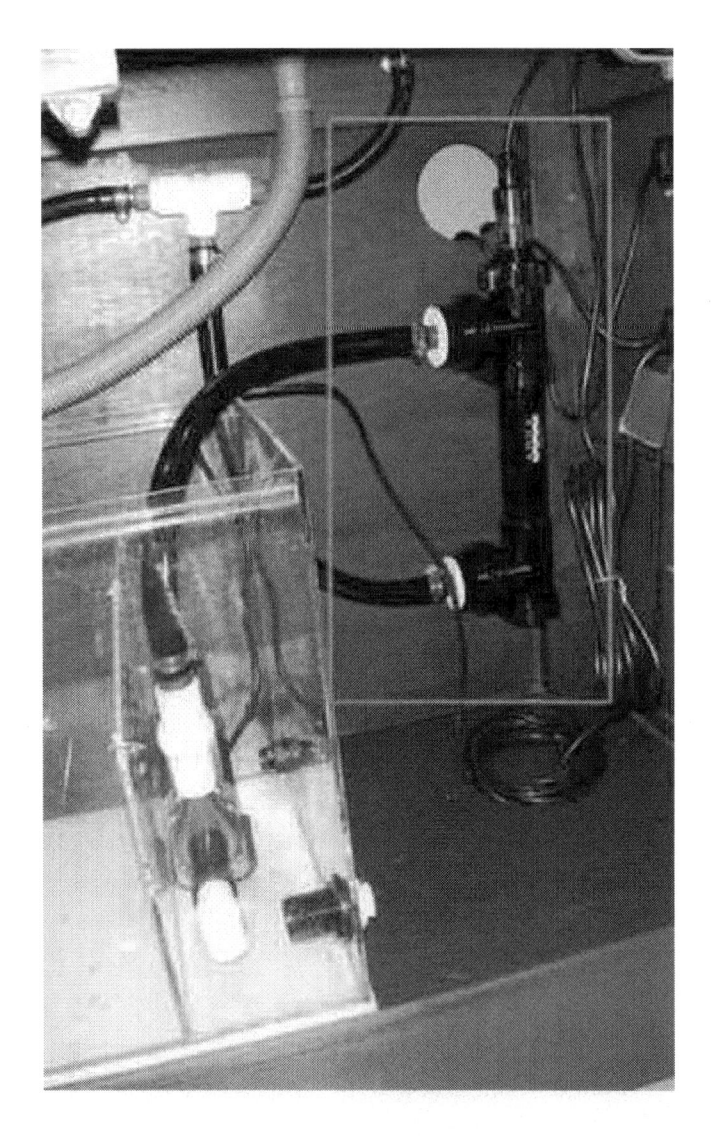

Inline UV sterilizer installed in aquarium stand

TIP: A UV light bulb needs to be changed on a regular basis. When installing an in-line UV, leave room to remove the light bulb or use clips which allows the UV sterilizer to tilt, to remove the light bulb.

Choosing and Stacking Live Rock

What is live rock and why use it?

Live rock is, as its name suggests, rock with living organisms (algae, bacteria, etc.) attached to it. Live rock comes from the ocean in different parts of the world such as Fiji, Marshall Islands, Tonga, Bali, Indo Pacific, and other tropical areas. It is usually named for the area in which it is found and harvested.

Fiji premium and Fiji shelf rock

Fiji branch and Fiji totoka

Fiji tukani and Real Reef Rock (manmade)

Many ecology-conscious entrepreneurs have begun to culture live rock by placing porous rock pieces on the ocean floor for a specified amount of time to allow algae, bacteria, animals and other organisms to grow in and on it. Whether natural or cultured, live rock brings natural biological properties from the ocean directly to your aquarium!

Some of the benefits of using live rock to aquascape your aquarium include the perhaps not so obvious biological benefits of increased surface area, and the introduction of helpful microorganisms, natural food sources, and living creatures that are found in the rock.

Is this live rock cured or uncured?

Live rock is removed from the ocean, placed in boxes and shipped through suppliers to aquarium stores. During shipping, much of the animal and plant life on the rock are damaged. When live rock is placed into an aquarium, the damaged and dying organisms create high levels of waste in the form of ammonia and nitrite, both of which are harmful to any live animals and plants that have survived the process.

Many pet and aquarium stores will take live rock from the ocean, "uncured" rock, through a process called "curing." If you choose to cure your own live rock see Appendix at the back of this guide.

Once the rock has gone through this process, it is called cured live rock. If possible, try to purchase cured rock and let the aquarium store suffer with the unavoidable rotten egg smell of the rock as it cures. Whether the rock you place in your aquarium is cured or uncured, it is important not to add any other animals until the ammonia and nitrite levels are zero. Uncured live rock takes 4 to 6 weeks before ammonia and nitrite levels return to zero. Cured rock may take a week or two before the levels drop.

TIP: Test ammonia and nitrite levels after adding live rock and before introducing fish. These levels must be zero before it is safe to add fish to your aquarium.

How much live rock do I need for my aquarium?

You can purchase live rock by the pound. The more porous the rock the lighter it is and the more surface area it has. Personal preference and the density of the rock will determine how many pounds are needed. If you have large fish or ones that need room to swim add a half to a pound of rock per gallon of aquarium water. If you want to create a large rockwork it typically requires one and a half to two pounds of rock per gallon of aquarium water.

Selecting live rock for your Aquarium

Choosing pieces to fit your tank

There are many ideas, preferences and opinions on how to aquascape with live rock. Some hobbyist prefer to place live rock flat across the bottom of the aquarium mimicking reef flat zones such as barrier reefs, atolls, fringes, or patch reefs. Others prefer to pile up rock in the center of their aquarium like islands mimicking outer reef edges like reef crests also known as shallow or upper reef slopes.

Stacking live rock

Another option is to stack rock high in the back of the aquarium simulating reef walls also known as fore reef slopes or deep reef slopes. This style is aesthetically pleasing, allowing the creation of large and small caverns for fish to swim through. It is versatile because it provides cliffs and areas on which to place live corals or a fish like the bicolor blenny to perch. This is the stacking method used in this book

In order to prepare to aquascape your aquarium choose a wide variety of pieces, as many different types of pieces as possible. Separate the pieces into three groups, which will be used to stack and aquascape the aquarium.

The groups are:
- Leg pieces (shaped like chair legs or cylinders), these pieces should be longer than they are wide and are used as legs to lift the main portion of the live rock off the substrate. These pieces should not be so wide as to take up a lot of surface area on the bottom of the aquarium.
- Flat pieces (shaped like platters or plates), are great for bridges, whether parallel or at an incline to provide slopes in the aquarium. These pieces lie across leg pieces connecting to other pieces creating the look of a reef cliff.
- Bulk pieces are wider, larger pieces, generally somewhat round and sometimes having arms extending from them or curved in crazy directions. These odd shapes are fundamental to use to make aquascaping creative. These can also be used as mid-level leg pieces creating 2nd level bridges. You can also use them for facial or frontal pieces providing bulk (or reality) to the edging pieces, slopes, or even as top bridge pieces. In this way, their roundness provides depth to the aquarium as well as reality to the height (as if it is actually the top of a ridge).

The order in which you add live rock, substrate and water can vary.

Option 1: First, stack live rock against the glass bottom of your aquarium and pour the substrate around the live rock. Finally add premixed saltwater.

Option 2: First add premixed saltwater or mix the saltwater inside the aquarium. Then stack live rock and pour the substrate around the rock.

Either of these techniques can ultimately lead to a successful saltwater and live rock aquarium. For the purpose of simplicity, this guide will explain the first technique in detail.

It is not a good idea to add substrate first because placing live rock on top of the substrate can make structures unstable. Some fish like to burrow and make tunnels and this can cause the rock to tumble. Stacking the rock first and pouring substrate around it creates a more stable structure, less susceptible to being toppled by the antics of burrowing creatures.

Stacking live rock on directly on bottom of aquarium

Stack rock in a sturdy fashion, yet loosely enough to keep water flowing through it. This will help your water quality. Also leave half to three-quarter of your substrate open (without rock covering it) to allow healthy water changes to pull out nutrients, organics and waste products from your aquarium. If you stack rock flat across the bottom of the tank or in the island fashion, it can be more difficult to extract waste from the substrate.

Whichever style of rock formation you choose here are a few rules to follow:
- Try to keep as much of the substrate open as possible.

- Make sure the rocks are stable. Use aquarium epoxy to help stabilize the rock.
- Build caves to allow the fish to feel relaxed.
- Use the rocks to hide filter and heaters to create a natural look.

It is interesting to note that live rock, pulled from the ocean, existed in a huge body of living, moving water. The ocean is what is called an open system, one in which water is constantly moving, washing away dirt, debris, nutrients, harmful chemicals, etc, and bringing in cleaner water. An aquarium is a closed system, one that does not have new water entering and old water exiting constantly. That is why we filter water in aquariums, to simulate the natural processes. In addition, we do water changes to remove wastes and debris.

Using Purified Water

Pure water is vital to the role in keeping our fish healthy. Reverse Osmosis (RO) and Reverse Osmosis with Deionization (RO/DI) is the preferred water for a reef. RO and RO/DI are processes used to clean city, municipal and well water using filter cartridges. Some hobbyist use city or municipal supplies however there are definite advantages to using RO and RO/DI.

Municipal and Well Water

Municipal water can contain chlorine or chloramines that must be neutralized before this water can be added to an aquarium. Besides chlorine compounds added by water treatment plants, there are many other impurities that can cause havoc to our living reef. Some of these impurities found in both municipal and well water include nitrates, phosphates, silicates, organic compounds, heavy metals and even toxins such as pesticides and fertilizers.

Nitrates, phosphates, and silicates are food for unwanted algae. Trying to keep algae under control in your reef when your water source is full of fertilizer (which causes algae to grow even faster than normal) can be very frustrating. Then there are the challenges caused by heavy metals. Trace amounts of some heavy metals are important for saltwater organisms to thrive, but as some levels increase, like copper for example, they can be fatal to corals, invertebrates and even fish. These are only a few of the risks that you take when using water straight from the tap. If you want to take control of the impurities in the water for your fish, use RO and RO/DI water.

Reverse Osmosis and Reverse Osmosis with Deionization

Reverse Osmosis (RO) and Reverse Osmosis with Deionization (RO/DI) are the purified waters of choice for most reef hobbyists. This water takes city or well water through a filtration process that removes 88% to 98% of the impurities. The process works by taking water through two pre-filter cartridges. One is a sediment cartridge to remove large debris; the other is a carbon cartridge to remove chlorine organic compounds and pesticides. Special cartridges are needed to remove chloramines. Water then passes through a semi-permeable membrane that is so dense that it allows only water molecules to pass through, leaving minerals, trace elements and other elements and compounds to be flushed away with wastewater. For each gallon of pure water that an RO unit produces, it also creates two to four gallons of wastewater.

Reverse osmosis system installed in cabinet

Reverse osmosis with deionization water filter installed under a home

Depending on the type of RO unit and the membrane used, as much as 92% dissolved solids water can be removed. Then, to get even cleaner water, some hobbyists add a deionization resin cartridge. After the water processes through the RO unit, it passes through the deionization resin and the resultant water is up to 98% pure.

Installing an RO unit in a home or office takes less than an hour. Some are even portable and can be attached directly to a faucet. If you choose not to purchase one, you can still purchase RO water at many aquarium stores. Just bring or buy containers to carry the water. If you ever question the purity of RO water, you can test it with a TDS meter, which indicates the level of total dissolved solids present. The lower the reading on the TDS meter the purer the water.

Remember, while a good salt mix is helpful, pure water makes all the difference!

TIP: Whether your budget allows you to get a top-of-the-line aquarium or you prefer to start with very basic equipment, the same principles apply across the board for water chemistry, water quality, keeping livestock, feeding, etc.

THE BIG DECISION!

To setup an UNDRILLED aquarium with live rock (FOWLR) go to **Chapter 2**

To setup an UNDRILLED aquarium with artificial decorations go to **Chapter 3**

To setup a DRILLED (Reef Ready) aquarium with live rock (FOWLR) go to **Chapter 4**

To setup a DRILLED (Reef Ready) aquarium with artificial decorations go to **Chapter 5**

Chapter 2

How to Assemble an Undrilled Aquarium with Live Rock (FOWLR)

This Chapter explains what is needed and how to set up a saltwater aquarium for fish and live rock. The process is slightly different from the procedure for a fish only saltwater aquarium.

Equipment and supplies with live rock

Basic Equipment

Start with an aquarium of at least 29-gallons. As a general rule, the larger the aquarium, the more stable the environment.

- Aquarium
- Aquarium stand

- Top with light
- Filter 6-8 times per gallon
- Heater 3-5W per gallon
- Thermometer
- Substrate
- Marine salt
- Hydrometer
- Artificial corals/plants (optional for color, variety)
- Live rock (1–1 1/2 lbs. / gallon aquarium water)
- Background
- De-chlorinator or water conditioner
- Bacteria starter
- Fish food
- 6-Outlet power strip

Optional Products
- Powerhead(s)
- Protein skimmer
- UV sterilizer
- Light timer
- Aquarium book

Testing Supplies
- pH test kit
- Ammonia test kit
- Nitrite test kit
- Nitrate test kit
- Syringe or dropper

Maintenance Supplies
- Gravel vacuum
- Algae scraper
- Algae magnet or sponge
- Salt mix

- Hydrometer
- Water conditioner
- Aquarium glass cleaner
- Towels
- Fish net
- Turkey baster
- Clean bucket to be used only for water changes

14 Steps to Setup Your New Live Rock Aquarium

Step 1: Choose a Location for Your Aquarium

Choose a location that is **out of direct sunlight**. Aquariums that receive direct sunlight usually grow an abundance of algae and while this is not harmful to fish, increased algae growth means more cleaning for you.

To keep your aquarium at a stable temperature place the aquarium away from heating or cooling ducts as well as doorways leading to the outside. Keeping it out of direct sunlight also helps keep the temperature stable.

Make certain you have an electrical outlet near the aquarium. Make sure your aquarium is spaced away from the wall allowing room to hang a filter on the back, if you are planning to use a hang on the back filter.

Finally, choose a room where you spend a lot of time and where you can sit down and enjoy your aquarium.

Step 2: Leveling Your Aquarium

If you are using an existing piece of furniture on which to place your new aquarium be sure it is level, sturdy and will handle the weight of the aquarium when full. Water weighs approximately 8.3 pounds per gallon. A 38 gallon aquarium full of water will weigh at least 315 pounds! Add to that the weight of the gravel, decorations and the glass itself and your aquarium is very heavy.

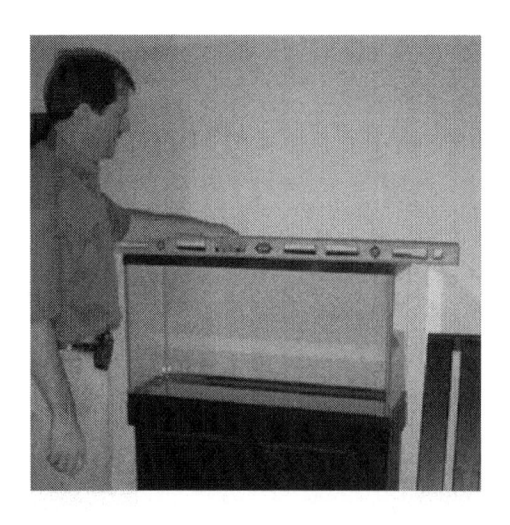

Make sure your aquarium is level front to back, side to side and corner to corner

Whether you have purchased an aquarium stand or are using existing furniture, be sure the base is level before you begin filling your aquarium. **Once the aquarium is filled with water, it will be obvious if the tank is not level.** This is not a good step on which to skimp.

Use a level. Level the aquarium front to back, side to side and corner to corner. Use shims under the stand at floor level until the tank is level. You may also purchase foam board to place between the aquarium and stand to absorb some of the imbalance if the rim of the stand can hide it.

Once shims are placed under the stand and the tank reads level, you are ready to move on.

NOTE: Level the stand with shims between the floor and the stand, not between the stand and the aquarium.

Step 3: Preparing the Aquarium

Using a soft cloth or damp paper towel, wipe down the inside of the aquarium to remove dirt and dust.

CAUTION: NEVER use soap or household cleaning agents in or on your aquarium. Even the most thorough rinse may not remove all chemicals left on the glass when using toxic cleaning products.

Step 4: Adding a Background

The background is attached to the outside back of the aquarium to hide the filter and electrical cords. It adds depth to your tank and can create a pleasing setting.

Attach background to outside of the aquarium

Clean and dry the back of the aquarium to prepare it for the background. Cut the background to the exact length of the aquarium. Use clear tape. Attach the right and left sides to your aquarium. Next, attach the top edge of the background with tape. Run a piece of tape the whole length of the top of the aquarium to keep water that may splash from the tank from forming spots between the background and the aquarium glass.

Step 5: Adding Filtration

There are several types of filters that can be used with a saltwater live rock and fish aquarium. The most commonly used is a power filter that hangs on the back of the aquarium. Canister filters or Berlin sumps can also be used with live rock as the rock surfaces contain bacteria that perform biological and chemical filtration.

Attaching the hang-on-filter to the back of the aquarium

Thus, when using live rock your filter needs to perform mechanical functions, removing particles from the water.

Since power filters are the most commonly used and inexpensive filters on the market today, we will use a power filter in our guide. If you are using another type of filter, please follow the manufacturer's directions.

Each brand of power filter is slightly different, with different shapes and features, but here are the general procedures to placing them on the aquarium:

Hang the filter on the back of the aquarium. Place the intake tube into the designated slot and place filter media in according manufacturer's instructions.

DO NOT plug the filter in at this time. After your aquarium is full of water, the filter may be started.

Step 6: Install Protein Skimmer

Protein skimmers physically remove dissolved organic compounds and other substances from aquarium water. Place the hang-on protein skimmer on the opposite side of the aquarium from the power filter as shown. **DO NOT plug it in at this time**.

Hanging protein skimmer on back of aquarium

Step 7: Install a Power Strip

It is always a safe idea to mount a power strip under the cabinet. Laying a power strip on the floor behind an aquarium stand is risky as there is then the chance that water could spill on it. Saltwater and electricity make a bad combination. If you have your aquarium sitting on top of a desk or shelf - make sure no water can ever splash on the power outlet or power strip.

Step 8: Adding Live Rock

What is live rock and why use it?

Live rock is, as its name suggests, rock with living organisms (algae, bacteria, etc.) attached to it. Live Rock comes from the ocean in different parts of the world such as Fiji, Marshall Islands, Tonga, Bali, Indo Pacific, and other tropical areas. It is usually named for the area in which it is found and harvested. Many ecology-conscious entrepreneurs have begun to culture live rock by placing porous rock pieces on the ocean floor for a specified amount of time to allow algae, bacteria, animals and other organisms to grow in and on it. Whether natural or cultured, live rock brings natural biological properties from the ocean directly to your aquarium!

Some of the benefits of using live rock to aquascape, i.e. decorate, your aquarium, include the perhaps not so obvious biological benefits of increased surface area, and the introduction of helpful microorganisms, natural food sources, and living creatures that are found in the rock.

Stacking live rock

Is This Live Rock Cured Or Uncured?

Live rock is removed from the ocean, placed in boxes and shipped through suppliers to aquarium stores. During shipping, much of the animal and plant life on the rock are damaged. When live rock is placed into an aquarium, the damaged and dying organisms create high levels of waste in the form of ammonia and nitrite, both of which are harmful to any live animals and plants that have survived the process.

Many pet and aquarium stores will take live rock from the ocean, "uncured" rock, through a process called "curing." Once the rock has gone through this process, it is called cured live rock. If possible, try to purchase cured rock and let the aquarium store suffer with the unavoidable rotten egg smell of the rock as it cures. Whether the rock you place in your aquarium is cured or uncured, it is important not to add any other animals until the ammonia and nitrite levels are zero. Uncured live rock takes 4 to 6 weeks before ammonia and nitrite levels return to zero. Cured rock may take a week, or two, before the levels drop.

TIP: Test ammonia and nitrite levels after adding live rock and before introducing fish. These levels must be zero before it is safe to add fish to your aquarium.

How Much Live Rock Do I need for my aquarium?

You can purchase live rock by the pound. The more porous the rock the lighter it is and the more surface area it has. It is a good rule of thumb to use 1 to 1 1/2 pounds of rock per gallon of aquarium water. Personal preference and the density of the rock will determine how many pounds are needed.

Selecting Live Rock for your Aquarium

Choosing pieces to fit your tank

There are many ideas, preferences and opinions on how to aquascape with live rock. Some prefer to place live rock flat across the bottom of the aquarium mimicking reef flat zones such as barrier reefs, atolls, fringes, or patch reefs. Others prefer to pile up rock in the center of their aquarium like islands mimicking outer reef edges like reef crests also known as shallow or upper reef slopes.

Completed stacking of live rock

Another option is to stack rock high in the back of the aquarium simulating reef walls also known as fore-reef slopes or deep reef slopes. This style is aesthetically pleasing, allowing the creation of large and/or small caverns for fish to swim through. It is versatile because if you choose to add live corals it provides cliffs and areas on which to stack them. It also allows you to place corals with regard to their needs, such as elevation, circulation, and lighting. This is the stacking method used in this book.

In order to prepare to aquascape your aquarium choose a wide variety of pieces, as many different types of pieces as possible, up to 1 1/2 lbs. of live rock per gallon of water. Separate the pieces into three groups, which will be used to stack and aquascape the aquarium.

The groups are:
- Leg pieces (shaped like chair legs or cylinders), these pieces should be longer than they are wide and are used as legs to lift the main portion of the live rock off the substrate. These pieces should not be so wide as to take up a lot of surface area on the bottom of the aquarium.

- Flat pieces (shaped like platters or plates), are great for bridges, whether parallel or at an incline to provide slopes in the aquarium. These pieces lie across leg pieces connecting to other pieces creating the look of a reef cliff.
- Bulk pieces are wider, larger pieces, generally somewhat round and sometimes having arms extending from them or curved in crazy directions. These odd shapes are fundamental to use to make aquascaping creative. These can also be used as mid-level leg pieces creating 2nd level bridges. You can also use them for facial or frontal pieces providing bulk (or reality) to the edging pieces, slopes, or even as top bridge pieces. In this way, their roundness provides depth to the aquarium as well as reality to the height (as if it is actually the top of a ridge).

The order in which you add live rock, substrate and water can vary.

Option 1: First, stack live rock against the glass bottom of your aquarium and pour the substrate around the live rock. Finally add premixed saltwater.

Option 2: First add premixed saltwater or mix the saltwater inside the aquarium. Then stack live rock and pour the substrate around the rock.

Either of these techniques can ultimately lead to a successful saltwater and live rock aquarium. For the purpose of simplicity, this guide will explain the first technique in detail.

It is not a good idea to add substrate first because placing live rock on top of the substrate can make structures unstable. Some fish like to burrow and make tunnels and this can cause the rock to tumble. Stacking the rock first and pouring substrate around it creates a more stable structure, less susceptible to being toppled by the antics of burrowing creatures.

Stack rock in a sturdy fashion, yet loosely enough to keep water flowing through it. This will help your water quality. Also leave 1/2 to 3/4 of your substrate open (without rock covering it) to allow healthy water changes to pull out nutrients, organics and waste products from your aquarium. If you stack rock flat across the bottom of the tank or in the island fashion, it can be more difficult to extract waste from the substrate.

Whichever style of rock formation you choose here are a few rules to follow:
- Try to keep as much of the substrate open as possible.
- Make sure the rocks are stable. Use aquarium epoxy to help stabilize the rock.
- Build caves to allow the fish to feel relaxed.
- Use the rocks to hide filter parts, heaters and to create a natural look.

It is interesting to note that live rock, pulled from the ocean, existed in a huge body of living, moving water. The ocean is what is called an open system, one in which water is constantly moving, washing away dirt, debris, nutrients, harmful chemicals, etc, and bringing in cleaner water. An aquarium is a closed system, one that does not have new water entering and old water exiting constantly. That is why we filter water in aquariums, to simulate the natural processes. In addition, we do water changes to remove wastes and debris.

Step 9: Adding Substrate

The substrate you choose should be made of aragonite, a beneficial substrate that slowly dissolves and releases buffers to help keep the pH at an ideal level for saltwater fish. Some substrates are clean and require no pre-rinsing. If the substrate you chose looks dusty or dirty simply rinse it in a large bucket, 10 to 15 pounds at a time. Run clean tap water through it, stir and drain it to wash away dust and debris. You may also use a kitchen colander. Some aquarists prefer thick substrate beds. For our purposes, we will add enough substrate to create a 1/2" to 1" thick layer.

Pouring in the substrate

Pour aragonite into an open spot on the floor of the aquarium. Then spread it evenly on the bottom of the aquarium to a depth of 1/2 to 1 inch thick.

Step 10: The Heater & Powerhead

There are two main styles of heaters. One style hangs on the back of the aquarium on the inside of the tank with the heater tube submersed and the controls above the water line, the other is fully submersible.

TIP: Whichever heater you choose, make sure that you have 3-5 watts per gallon of water. A 29-gallon tank uses at least a 100-Watt heater.

Submersible heaters are best for saltwater aquariums. For most submersible heaters, just set the dial to a specific temperature and a thermostat inside the heater will keep the temperature constant. Because there are many manufacturers, it is best to follow their specific instructions to set and attach your heater. **DO NOT plug the heater in to an outlet at this point.**

Set the temperature between 80° and 82°F for the first 4 to 6 weeks (until a biological foundation is established). Once your aquarium is cycled, (More information about the cycle can be found in Water Quality Explained) set the temperature to between 74° and 78°F.

Powerhead installation: Powerheads help circulate water and increase the current in the aquarium; they keep water flowing through the live rock, reminiscent of the flow of water in the ocean.

Powerheads can be installed on the side or back panes of glass, on either or both sides of the aquarium.

Recap:
Step 1: Choose location
Step 2: Level stand
Step 3: Rinse aquarium
Step 4: Add background
Step 5: Add hang filter
Step 6: Install protein skimmer
Step 7: Install electrical power strip
Step 8: Add live rock
Step 9: Add aragonite
Step 10: Attach heater and powerhead

DO NOT plug power outlet strip into wall receptacle at this time.

Step 11: Adding Water

NOTE: Below is an explanation of how to mix salt water at home although my preference is to use RO (Reverse Osmosis) water. This water, often found sold by 5-gallon jugs at local fish and pet stores, is sent through a series of filters which remove most of the impurities, particularly phosphates and nitrates. This helps significantly to control algae! (More information on RO water can be found in Chapter 1.)

For smaller aquariums (up to 45-gallons), several five gallon buckets filled at the kitchen or bathtub faucet are all you will need to fill the tank.

Adding premixed saltwater

For larger aquariums, carrying water back and forth may take too much time and energy. You may want to purchase a new thirty-five to forty-five gallon trashcan or other food-grade container. Rubbermaid brand plastic containers are made of non-toxic material. Whichever size bucket you choose it should be used only for your aquarium.

CAUTION: When using a live rock and live sand substrate you MUST mix the salt and water before adding it to the aquarium. If you add freshwater directly to your live sand, you can kill the beneficial bacteria in the sand.

Since you are using live rock, you must premix your saltwater before adding it to the aquarium.

Begin by filling a bucket with water at a temperature of 82°F. Use hot and cold water until you achieve the final temperature. Next, add salt to the water. Follow the instructions on the salt mix you purchased, keeping in mind that a general rule is to add one cup of salt to every two gallons of aquarium water.

After mixing salt with the water in the bucket, use a hydrometer to test specific gravity. There are two different types of hydrometers that aquarists use. One is a plastic box with a floating swing-arm and the other looks similar to a floating glass thermometer. Either style will work.

The specific gravity should read between 1.020 and 1.025. If the specific gravity is too low, add more salt. If you add too much salt and the hydrometer reads over the target, remove some of the water and add fresh water.

Once your saltwater mix is ready, add a good de-chlorinator to each bucket to remove chlorine allowing you to safely add the saltwater mix to the aquarium with live sand. If your water has chloramines, add a water conditioner like Sachem's Prime®.

Test pH and make sure it is between 8.0 and 8.4. If the pH is below 8.0, add a buffering agent to adjust it. (More information about pH can be found in Water Quality Explained)

Pour water slowly onto one of the live rocks close to the bottom of the aquarium. (Since you just spread out the substrate, you do not want to blow it all around.) You might want to place a dinner plate in the aquarium temporarily on which to pour the water. Fill the aquarium until the water level is just above the bottom of the aquarium's frame.

Step 12: Starting the Equipment

Rinse the filter cartridge and fill the filter compartment with water to prime it.

Plug the filter in to an electrical outlet. Water will be drawn up the intake tube and the filter will fill with aquarium water. Once full, water will spill back into the aquarium.

Plug in the protein skimmer.

Make sure the filter and protein skimmer are running

Install a Thermometer

Attach a hanging thermometer to the aquarium on the side opposite the heater, about three inches from the top of the aquarium. Keep a thermometer in the aquarium as it allows you to ensure the heater works properly and, during the warm months, it helps you keep tabs that the aquarium is not getting too hot.

> *NOTE: A thermometer is also necessary for water changes. When you change aquarium water, you want to make sure the new water is within 2 degrees of the temperature of the water in your aquarium.*

Plug in the Heater

Once the water is in the aquarium, wait ten to fifteen minutes before plugging in the heater to allow the temperature of the heater's glass tube to acclimate to the temperature of the water. This will prevent the glass tube from cracking due to a rapid change in temperature.

> *SAFETY TIP: Make sure any electrical wires leading from your filter, heater, and lights to an electrical outlet have drip loops. If a drop of water travels down your cord it will*

drip at the bottom of the loop before it enters your electrical socket. Electrical cords, when plugged into the electrical outlet, must loop below the outlet.

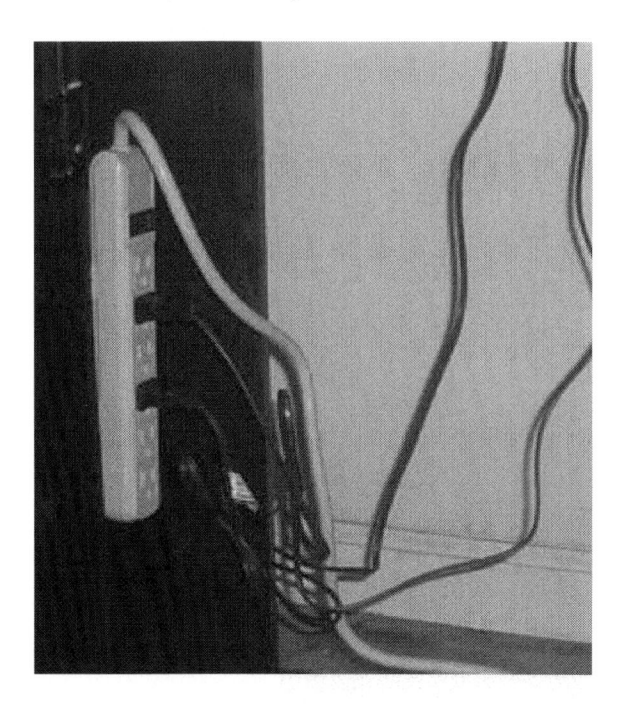

Electrical cords with drip loop

Step 13: Placing the Top and Light

Cut openings for the filter in the plastic part of your hood or glass top. The openings should correspond with filter placement. Some plastic aquarium hoods have optional cutouts that you just break off with pliers, you are limited somewhat on where to place the filter; glass tops come with a strip of plastic attached to the back glass, which can be cut with sturdy scissors.

Place the hood or glass tops on the aquarium, set the strip light on the glass tops, plug it in and turn on the light.

Lights should stay on between 6 and 10 hours each day. For example, if you are home in the evenings you can have your lights on from noon until 10 pm at night. It is best to run lights during the day and turn them off at night. If the light remains on 24 hours a day, you will probably grow immense amounts of algae.

TIP: Use an appliance timer to turn aquarium lights on and off at the same time each day.

Step 14: The Final Step

Put a canopy (if you have one) on the aquarium; stand back and enjoy your creation!

Competed live rock setup

Aquarium decorated with live rock and dotted with colorful, artificial, corals and marine plants

Many artificial decorations look very lifelike. These decorations are a great way to add a splash of color to your live rock decor.

It is your aquarium if you like just the live rock great or you can decorate the aquarium the way you like it.

Once the live rock has cycled (discussed in "Water Quality Explained", Chapter 6), you are ready to do a partial water change and add some livestock.

Chapter 3

How to Assemble an Undrilled Aquarium with Artificial Decorations

Equipment and supplies with artificial decorations

Basic Equipment:
Start with an aquarium of at least 29 gallons. As a general rule, the larger the aquarium, the more stable the environment.
- Aquarium
- Aquarium stand
- Top with light
- Filter 6-8 times per gallon
- Heater 3-5W per gallon
- Thermometer
- Substrate
- Marine salt

- Hydrometer
- Artificial corals
- Artificial plants
- Background
- De-chlorinator or water conditioner
- Bacteria starter
- Fish food
- 6-Outlet power strip

Optional Products
- Powerhead(s)
- Protein skimmer
- UV sterilizer
- Light timer

Testing Supplies
- pH test kit
- Ammonia test kit
- Nitrite test kit
- Nitrate test kit
- Syringe or dropper

Maintenance Supplies
- Gravel vacuum
- Algae scraper
- Algae magnet or sponge
- Salt mix
- Hydrometer
- Water conditioner
- Aquarium glass cleaner
- Towels
- Fish net
- Clean bucket to be used only for water changes

15 Steps to Setting Up Your Aquarium

Step 1: Choose a Location for Your Aquarium

Choose a location that is **out of direct sunlight**. Aquariums that receive direct sunlight usually grow an abundance of algae and while this is not harmful to fish, increased algae growth means more cleaning for you.

To keep your aquarium at a stable temperature place the aquarium away from heating or cooling ducts as well as doorways leading to the outside. Keeping it out of direct sunlight also helps keep the temperature stable.

Make certain you have an electrical outlet near the aquarium. Make sure your aquarium is spaced away from the wall allowing room to hang a filter on the back, if you are planning to use a hang on the back filter.

Finally, choose a room where you spend a lot of time and where you can sit down and enjoy your aquarium.

Step 2: Level Your Aquarium

If you are using an existing piece of furniture on which to place your new aquarium be sure it is level, sturdy and will handle the weight of the aquarium when full. Water weighs approximately 8.3 pounds per gallon. A 38 gallon aquarium full of water will weigh at least 315 pounds! Add to that the weight of the gravel, decorations and the glass itself and your aquarium is very heavy.

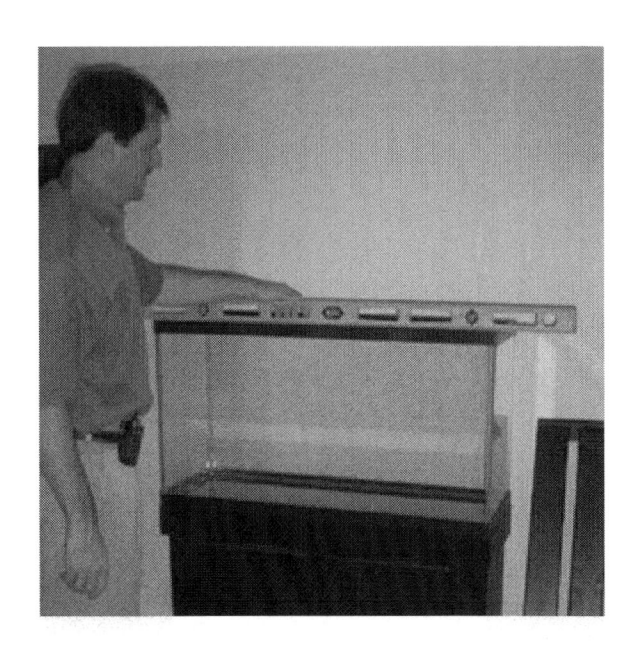

Make sure your aquarium is level front to back side to side and corner to corner

Whether you have purchased an aquarium stand or are using existing furniture, be sure the base is level before you begin filling your aquarium. **Once the aquarium is filled with water, it will be obvious if the tank is not level.** This is not a good step on which to skimp.

Use a level. Level the aquarium front to back, side to side and corner to corner. Use shims under the stand at floor level until the tank is level. You may also purchase foam board to place between the aquarium and stand to absorb some of the imbalance if the rim of the stand can hide it.

Once shims are placed under the stand and the tank reads level, you are ready to move on.

NOTE: Level the stand with shims between the floor and the stand, not between the stand and the aquarium.

Step 3: Preparing the Aquarium

Using a soft cloth or damp paper towel, wipe down the inside of the aquarium to remove dirt and dust.

Clean inside of aquarium with water only

CAUTION: NEVER use soap or household cleaning agents in or on your aquarium. Even the most thorough rinse may not remove all chemicals left on the glass when using toxic cleaning products.

Step 4: Adding a Background

The background is attached to the outside back of the aquarium to hide the filter and electrical cords. It adds depth to your tank and can create a pleasing setting.

Clean and dry the back of the aquarium to prepare it for the background. Cut the background to the exact length of the aquarium.

Use clear tape. Attach the right and left sides to your aquarium. Next, attach the top edge of the background with tape. Run a piece of tape the whole length of the top of the aquarium to keep water that may splash from the tank from forming spots between the background and the aquarium glass.

Step 5: Adding Substrate

The substrate (gravel) you choose should be made of aragonite.

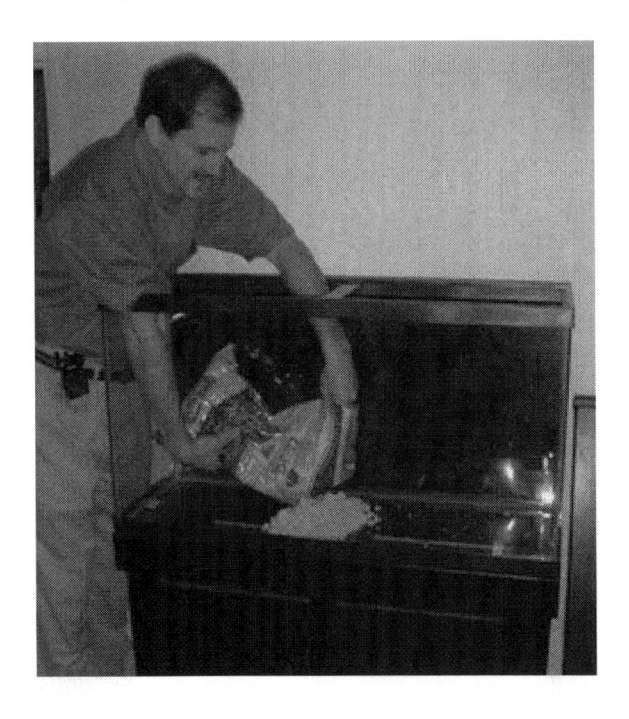

Pouring in the substrate

Aragonite is a beneficial substrate that slowly dissolves and releases buffers to help keep pH at an ideal level for saltwater fish. Many substrates today are clean and require no pre-rinsing (live sand is packed in water with living bacteria and should NOT be rinsed.) If the dry substrate you chose looks dusty or dirty simply rinse it in a large bucket, 10 to 15 pounds at a time. Run clean tap water through it, stir and drain it to wash away dust and debris. You may also use a kitchen colander. Add enough substrate to create a 1/2" to 1" thick layer in a fish-only aquarium.

Step 6: Adding Filtration

There are several types of filters that can be used with a saltwater aquarium. The most common are power filters that hang on the back of the aquarium. Canister filters and wet/dry or trickle filters are also popular.

Attaching the hang-on-filter to the back of the aquarium

TIP: Whichever brand filter you choose, it should be able to turn your aquarium water 5 to 8 times per hour. A 29-gallon aquarium needs a filter that will turn between 145 to 232 gallons per hour.

Since power filters are the most common filters currently used, we will discuss these. If you are using another type of filter, please follow the manufacturer's directions.

Each brand of power filter is slightly different, with different shapes and features, but here are the general procedures to placing them on the aquarium:

Hang the filter on the back of the aquarium. Place the intake tube into the designated slot and place filter media in according manufacturer's instructions.

DO NOT plug the filter in at this time. After your aquarium is full of water, the filter may be started.

Step 7: Attaching a Heater

There are two main styles of heaters. One style hangs on the back of the aquarium on the inside of the tank while the other is fully submersible.

Submersible heaters are best for saltwater aquariums. Most submersible heaters allow you to set a dial to a specific temperature and a thermostat inside the heater keeps the temperature constant. Since there are many manufacturers of submersible heaters, it is best to follow the manufacturers' instructions to set and attach your heater.

DO NOT plug the heater in at this point. Set the temperature between 80° and 82°F for the first 4 to 6 weeks (until a biological foundation is established and the aquarium is cycled). Once your aquarium is cycled, set the temperature to 74° - 78°.

TIP: Whichever heater you choose, make sure that you have 3-5 watts per gallon of aquarium water. A 29-gallon tank uses at least a 100-Watt heater.

Step 8: Decorating Your Aquarium

Decorate your aquarium as you please. There are no hard, fast rules. We are all individuals and have our own tastes, have fun and decorate until you are happy with the outcome. Some people like very sparse decorations; just be aware that **fish need to feel safe as if they are in their natural environment. They need hiding places to feel secure**. A tank with too few decorations is to your fish as a room with just sparse furniture is to most people.

Placing the decorations

Here are a few decorating suggestions to help you get started:

First, place the largest pieces of artificial coral a little towards the back of the aquarium. As you place the decorations, think of ways to hide the heater and filter intake tubes. If you have three large pieces of coral decorations you can place them in a V shape where the right and left pieces are placed more to the back and the one in the center is placed toward the middle of the aquarium.

Place smaller pieces of coral randomly around your aquarium.

It is a good idea to place artificial plants close to the coral to leave some room for fish to swim. If you have plants that are the same type but different heights, place them near each other to give a natural effect of plants growing.

Tall plants are also great for hiding heaters and filter intake tubes. When placing tall plants in the aquarium, use the tallest near the back or sides of the aquarium. Tall plants will stand out and can be placed near structures and caves. Alternatively, put a large plant alone in the center of your tank and add smaller plants around it.

Use medium sized plants in front of larger plants to provide a feeling of different levels, to add color and depth, and to enlarge the bigger plant to make it look fuller.

Finally yet importantly, place your short plants. These plants are the final pieces to your masterpiece. Use them as abstract pieces for color or size and place them between, in front of, or just around other decorations in your aquarium.

The best part about decorating is to simply have fun. If you finish and want to make changes, go ahead.

Recap:
Step 1: Choose location
Step 2: Level stand
Step 3: Rinse aquarium
Step 4: Add background
Step 5: Add aragonite
Step 6: Hang filter
Step 7: Attach heater
Step 8: Decorate

Step 9: Adding Water

For smaller aquariums (up to 40-gallons), several five gallon buckets filled at the kitchen or bathtub faucet are all you will need to fill the tank.

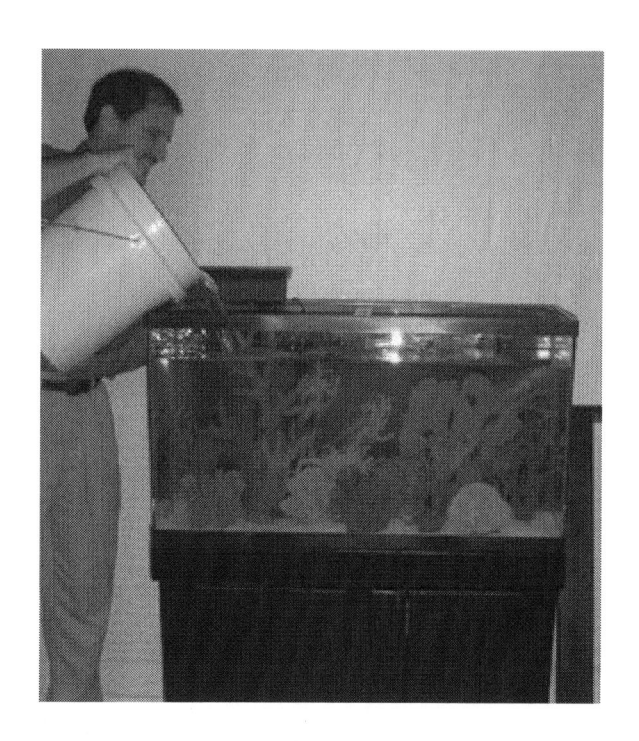

Adding premixed saltwater

For larger aquariums, carrying water back and forth may take too much time and energy. You may want to get a new trashcan or food-grade container that holds from thirty-five to forty-five gallons. Rubbermaid brand plastic cans are made of non-toxic material and offer an attachment with wheels to make movement easier. Whichever size bucket you choose it should be used only for your aquarium.

CAUTION: When using a live sand substrate you MUST mix the salt and water before adding it to the aquarium. If you add freshwater directly to your live sand, you can kill the beneficial bacteria in the sand.

How to Fill Your Aquarium With Saltwater

Mix salt and water in buckets **before** adding it to your aquarium. Begin by filing a bucket with water at a temperature of 82°F. Use hot and cold water until you achieve the final temperature. Now add salt to the water, following instructions on the salt mix you chose. The general rule is to add one cup of salt to every two gallons of aquarium water.

After the salt dissolves in the water in the bucket, use a hydrometer to test specific gravity. There are two popular types of hydrometers. One is a plastic box with a floating swing-arm and the other looks similar to a floating glass thermometer. Either style will work. You want the hydrometer to read a specific gravity between 1.020 and 1.025. If the specific gravity reads too low, add more salt. If you add too much salt and the hydrometer reads over the target then remove some of the salt water and add fresh water.

Once your saltwater mix is ready, add a good de-chlorinator or water conditioner to each bucket. (De-chlorinators remove chlorine, making it safe to add your saltwater mix to your live sand. Your water may have chloramines. Buy a water conditioner that removes chloramines.)

Pour the mixed water onto a large decoration or a dinner plate that you place temporarily in the aquarium. This keeps the substrate from blowing around when you pour the water. Fill the aquarium until the water level is just above the bottom of the aquarium's frame.

CAUTION: If the aquarium glass is cold DO NOT ADD HOT WATER or the glass will crack!

NOTE: While explaining how to mix salt water at home, my preference is to use RO (Reverse Osmosis) water. This water, often sold in five-gallon jugs at local fish and pet stores, is forced through a series of filters that remove most impurities including phosphates and nitrates. This helps significantly to control algae! (More information on RO water is found in Chapter 1.)

Step 10: Install a Thermometer

Attach a hanging thermometer to the aquarium on the side opposite the heater, about three inches from the top of the aquarium.

Keeping a thermometer in the aquarium allows you to make sure the heater is working properly. During warm months, it helps you keep tabs that the aquarium is not getting too hot.

NOTE: A thermometer is also necessary for water changes. When changing aquarium water, you want to make sure the new water is within 2 degrees of the temperature of the water in your aquarium.

Step 11: Install a Power Strip

It is a safe idea to mount the power strip under the cabinet. Laying a power strip on the floor behind an aquarium stand is risky as there is then a chance that water could spill onto the power strip. Saltwater and electricity are a bad combination. If you have your aquarium sitting on top of a desk or shelf, make sure no water can ever splash on the power outlets.

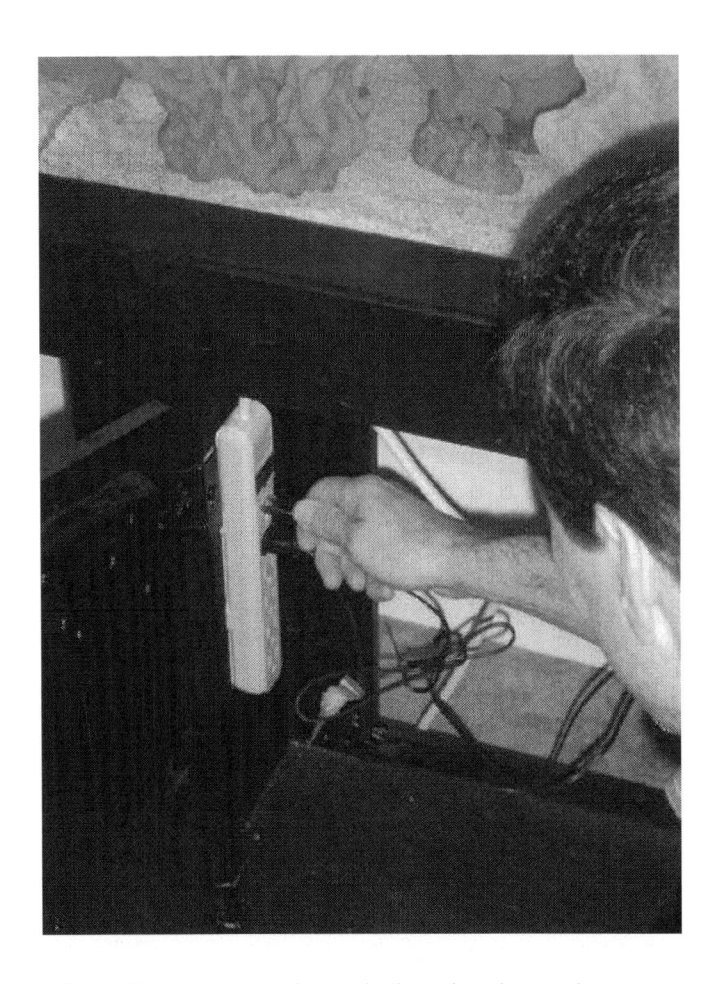

Installed power strip and plugging in equipment

Step 12: Start the Filter

Rinse the filter cartridge and fill the filter compartment at least half way with water from the aquarium to prime it. Make sure the intake tube is in place, it should drop easily and firmly into a slot over the impeller. Now plug in the filter. Aquarium water will be drawn up the intake tube, the filter will fill up and water will then spill back into the aquarium.

Step 13: Plug in the Heater

Once the water is in the aquarium, wait ten to fifteen minutes before plugging in the heater. This allows the temperature of the glass tube to acclimate to the temperature of the water, preventing the glass tube from cracking due to a rapid change in temperature.

> *SAFETY TIP: Make sure any electrical wires leading from your filter, heater, and lights to an electrical outlet have drip loops. If a drop of water travels down your cord it will drop off at the bottom of the loop before it enters your electrical socket. Electrical cords, when plugged into the electrical outlet, must loop below the outlet.*

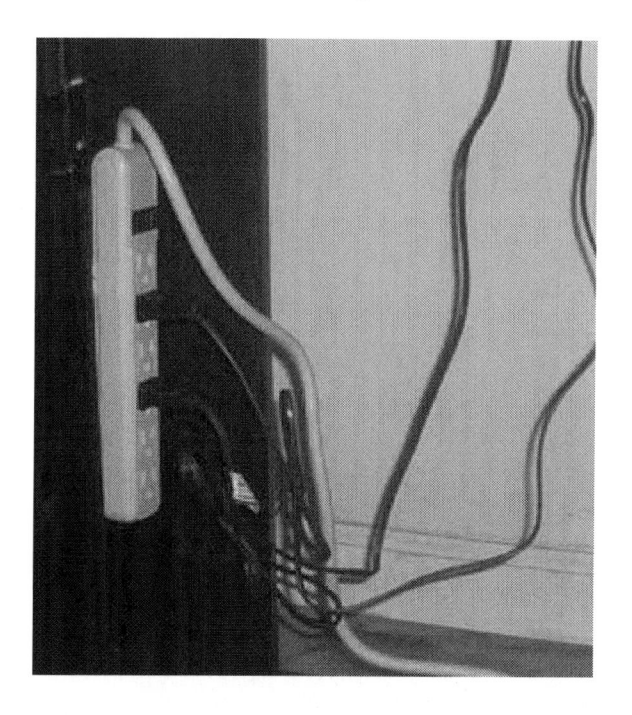

Electrical cords with drip loop

Step 14: Placing the Top and Light

Cut openings for the filter in the plastic part of your hood or glass top. The openings should correspond with your filter placement. Place the hood or glass tops on the aquarium, set the strip light over the glass, plug it in and turn on the light.

The lights should stay on from 6 to 10 hours each day. For example, if you are home in the evenings you can have your lights on from noon until 10 pm at night. It is best to run lights during the day and turn them off at night. If the light remains on 24 hours a day, you will probably grow immense amounts of algae.

Tip: Use an appliance timer to turn the aquarium lights on and off at the same time each day

Step 15: The Final Step

Place the canopy on the aquarium, if you have one.

Completed saltwater set up with artificial decorations

Stand back and enjoy!

At this point, your aquarium is completely setup. Now is the perfect time to learn about water quality in Chapter 6.

Chapter 4

How to Assemble a Drilled Aquarium with Live Rock (FOWLR)

This is the fun part: the actual aquarium assembly! And we are one step closer to adding our aquatic friends.

First, look at the equipment necessary to build our saltwater aquarium. Next, check out some optional products and finally, find a list of necessary test kits.

Basic Equipment:
- Aquarium, drilled with overflow (at least 75 gallons)
- Aquarium stand
- Top with light or canopy
- Berlin sump or Berlin sump with refugium
- Return water pump
- Powerhead(s)
- Protein skimmer
- UV sterilizer
- Submersible heater
- Thermometer
- Substrate
- Marine salt
- Live rock (1 1/2 - 2 lbs. / gallon of aquarium water)
- Background (optional)
- Reverse osmosis water
- Bacteria starter
- 6-outlet power strip(s)
- Light timer(s)

Optional Products
- RO/DI filter System
- Wavemaker

Test Kits and Equipment
- Hydrometer
- pH test kit
- Ammonia test kit
- Nitrite test kit
- Nitrate test kit
- Syringe or dropper (optional)

Setting Up Your Saltwater Aquarium

Step 1: Choose a Location for Your Aquarium

Choose a location that is **out of direct sunlight**. Aquariums that receive direct sunlight usually grow an abundance of algae and while this is not harmful to fish, invertebrates or corals, increased algae growth means more cleaning for you.

To keep your aquarium at a stable temperature, place the aquarium away from heating or cooling ducts as well as doorways leading to the outside. Keeping it out of direct sunlight also helps keep the temperature stable.

Aquarium with black end overflow on left allows viewing from front, back and right end

Make certain you have an electrical outlet near the aquarium.

NOTE: Many high tech and large mini reef aquariums use a lot of current and may need their own dedicated circuit.

Choose a room where you spend a lot of time and where you can sit down and enjoy your aquarium.

Step 2: Leveling Your Aquarium

If you are using an existing piece of furniture on which to place your new aquarium be sure it is level, sturdy and will handle the weight of the aquarium when full. Water weighs approximately 8.3 pounds per gallon. A 90 gallon aquarium full of water will weigh at least 750 pounds! Add that 750 pounds to the weight of the substrate, live rock and the glass and this is a very heavy aquarium.

Make sure your aquarium is level front to back, side-to-side and corner-to-corner

Whether you have purchased an aquarium stand or are using existing furniture, be sure the base is level before you begin filling your aquarium. Once the aquarium is filled with water, it will be obvious if the tank is not level. This is not a good step on which to skimp.

Use a level. Level the aquarium front to back, side to side and corner to corner. Use shims (wooden or plastic wedges) under the stand at floor level until the tank is level.

NOTE: Level the stand with shims between the floor and the stand, never between the stand and the aquarium.

When installing the aquarium on carpet most of the time wood or metal strips are used to secure the carpet and keep it flat. These strips are installed close to a wall. If the aquarium is placed on a strip, it will raise up the back of the aquarium. If possible, space the aquarium from the wall in front of the strip.

Once shims are placed under the stand and the tank reads level, you are ready to move on.

Step 3: Preparing the Aquarium

Using a soft cloth or damp paper towel, wipe down the inside of the aquarium to remove dirt and dust.

CAUTION: NEVER use soap or household cleaning agents in or on your aquarium. Even the most thorough rinse may not remove all chemicals left on the glass when using toxic cleaning products.

Step 4: Adding a Background

The background is attached to the outside back of the aquarium to hide the filter and electrical cords. It adds depth to your tank and can create a pleasing setting. Clean and dry the back of the aquarium to prepare it for the background. Cut the background to the exact length of the aquarium. Use clear tape. Attach the right and left sides to your aquarium. Next, attach the top edge of the background with tape. Run a piece of tape the whole length of the top of the aquarium to keep water that may splash from the tank from forming spots between the background and the aquarium glass.

Step 5: Install Plumbing Kit in Overflow Box

Predrilled aquariums have at least two holes drilled in the bottom. One hole is plumbed to drain water from the aquarium and the other hole is plumbed to return water to the aquarium. These holes are enclosed in the aquarium by an overflow box. For additional information, see Chapter 2.

Our example uses an aquarium with the overflow attached to the back glass of an aquarium.

Back view of aquarium with overflow box and two holes in bottom of aquarium (not visible)

It is time to install the plumbing in the drain and return holes. Most aquarium manufacturers have overflow plumbing kits. Here is an example of the plumbing.

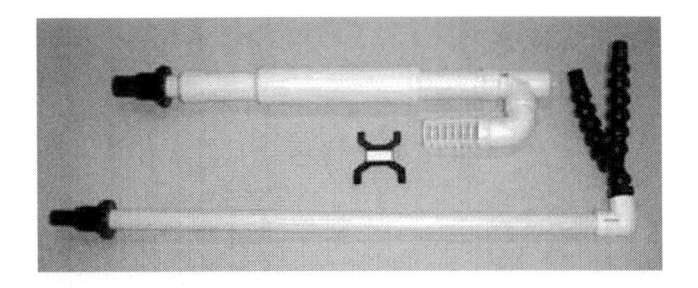

Drain and return assembly

Since each aquarium manufacturer has a different plumbing kit, just follow their directions to assemble and install in the aquarium.

Here is a finished view of drain and return installed.

Return assembly (thinner white tube on left) and drain assembly (larger white tube on right) installed

Step 6: Installing Filtration

A mini reef aquarium with live rock should use a Berlin filter. A Berlin filter has a sump (holding chamber) with a mechanical filter and space for a protein skimmer and other equipment. A Berlin filter is placed below the aquarium usually in a cabinet stand.

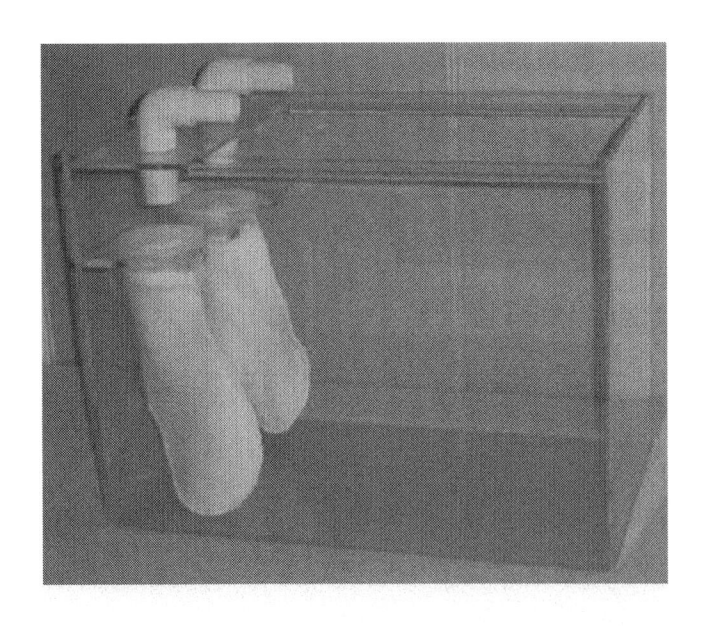

Basic - Berlin sump with 2 sock hangers and filter socks

Deluxe - Berlin sump has two sock hangers, refugium, protein skimmer and return water pump compartments

Place filter below aquarium in cabinet.

Placing Berlin sump in cabinet

TIP: A piece of Styrofoam placed under a Berlin sump will allow the filter to level itself and remove any unevenness from the stand.

The aquarium has its overflow plumbing kits installed and the filter is in the cabinet below the aquarium. Let's look at how the aquarium and filter work together.

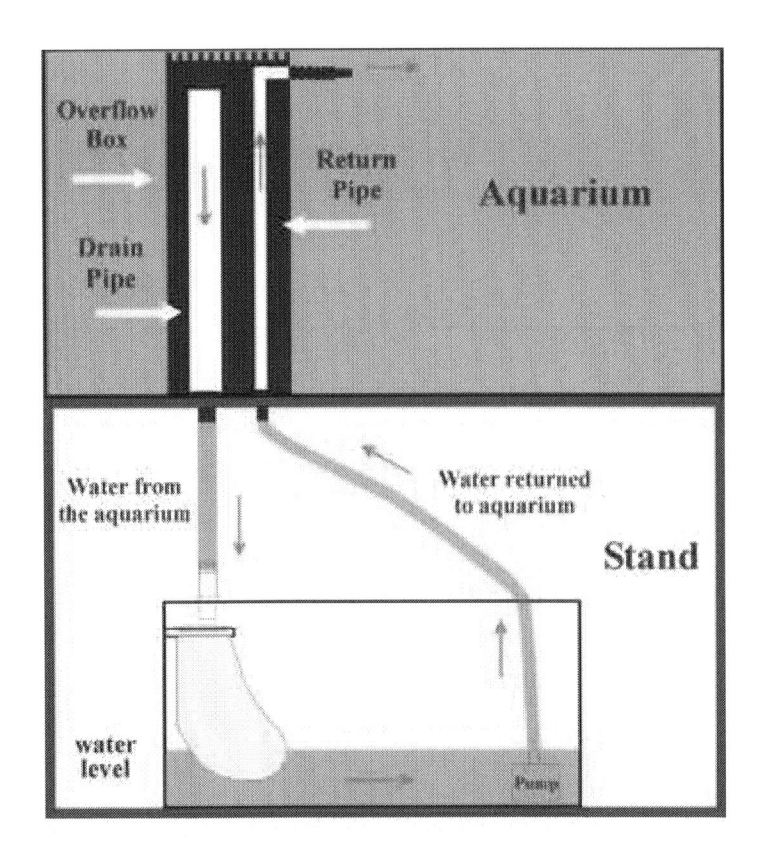

Diagram of installed Berlin sump and water flow

    This diagram shows how water is routed from the overflow box of the aquarium through a drain line down to the Berlin filter. It is pre-filtered through a filter sock and returned to the aquarium via a water pump.

    Here is the general way to install a Berlin sump. Berlin sumps typically have one or two connections on the top of the sump designed to be attached to the drain line(s) of your drilled aquarium.

Two vacuum hoses attached to Berlin filter

If you are using pre-manufactured drain lines such as vacuum hose, position the sump inside your cabinet so that the drain lines form as straight path as possible from the bottom of your overflow chamber to the drain line connections on the top of your sump.

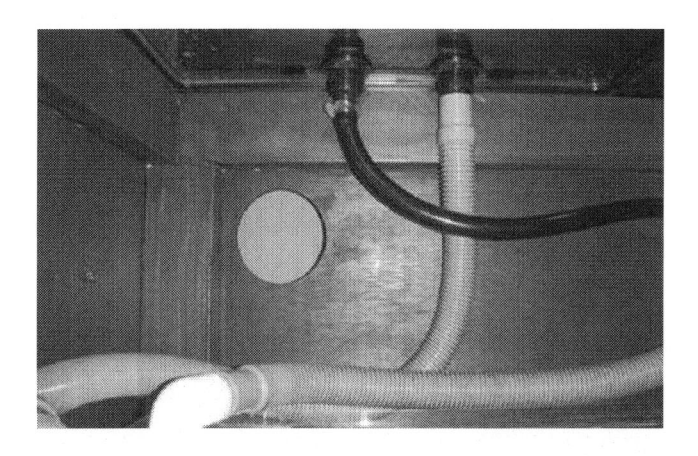

Gray vacuum line attached to drain line from aquarium

These drain lines should not drop below the top of the Berlin sump before connecting to the sump, as debris and air can collect in these areas and interfere with proper drainage from the aquarium. If your drain line is too long to make a straight path from the overflow bulkhead to your sump, loop the drain line in such a manner as to ensure water is always traveling down toward your sump.

Most pre-manufactured drain lines are made to fit one-inch PVC attachments on the top of sumps, and can be pressure fit to the drainage attachment on the sump. Because these lines are not under pressure, it is not necessary to use hose clamps. But, it never hurts to secure a hose clamp to all tubing.

Once the drain line is securely attached to the Berlin filter and the drain bulkhead of your display tank, the drainage of your aquarium to the Berlin filter is complete.

Step 7: Installing the Return Pump

Overflow boxes skim water off the surface of an aquarium and channel the water down to a Berlin filter. A pump then returns the water to your aquarium. The pump can be internal (placed inside the sump) or external (outside the sump).

Installing your return pump and plumbing is largely dependent upon your particular sump and configuration.

Internal Water Pump

Internal pumps have a return outlet that is either threaded or slip. This means you can thread a plastic fitting onto the threaded outlet or attach flexible tubing to the slip outlet. If your pump is a little too powerful for your aquarium a ball valve may be used to adjust the water flow. Threaded fittings on a pump make it convenient to thread a ball valve directly to the pump. Use Teflon tape on all the threads to make a waterproof seal. Once the ball valve is attached choose the size fitting you will need to run your return tubing back to your aquarium. If your aquarium has a bulkhead to return the water to your aquarium then make sure your flexible tubing is the correct size.

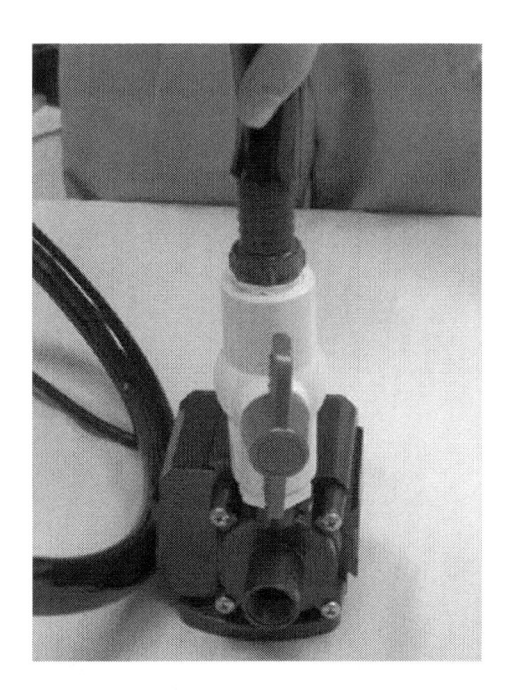

Internal pump with ball valve, poly fitting and flexible tubing

Make sure your flexible tubing attaches to your return fittings. Make your return line as straight as possible. The more bends increases the head pressure therefore reducing the water flow from the pump.

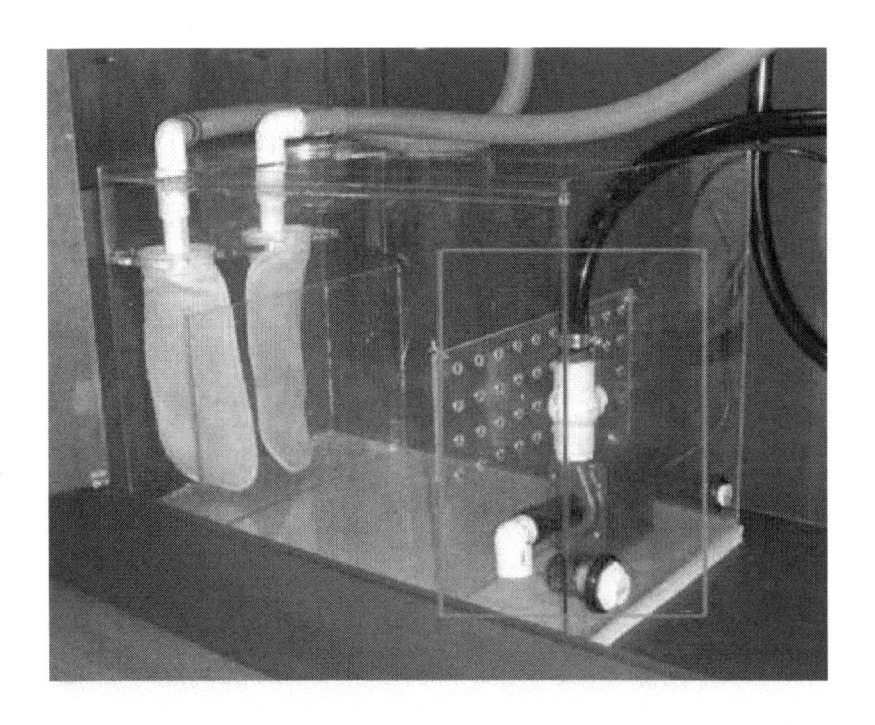

Internal water pump in sump on right

One side of the flexible tubing is attached to the pump the other side attaches to the return line sticking out the bottom of the aquarium.

Grey tubing attached to bulkhead drain from aquarium; water pump attached to right water return

External Water Pump

An external pump should be placed on a flat, dry surface next to the sump. If the pump does not have a rubber pad or feet then place a small layer of rubber or foam under the pump to minimize vibration. Some sumps come pre-drilled to accommodate external pump. Others, you must use a hole saw and drill your own hole. Just use a bulkhead to slide through the hole in the filter to attach an external pump.

If using a bulkhead then you can use either PVC fittings with flexible tubing or you may choose to plumb with standard PVC pipe and fittings.

External pump plumbed into a Berlin filter

TIP: To make it easy to remove or change an external water pump, use a true union ball valve between the intake side or the pump and the filter and another true union ball valve between the output side of the pump and the return tubing (not shown).

Step 8: Install an Ultraviolet Sterilizer (recommend option)

UV sterilizers are designed to hang on the back of an aquarium or plumbed-in-line between your filter's return pump and your aquarium. This ensures that 100 percent of the water that passes through the sump also goes through the UV. Make sure the UV sterilizer and the return pump are the proper size for your aquarium.

40 Watt in Inline UV sterilizer

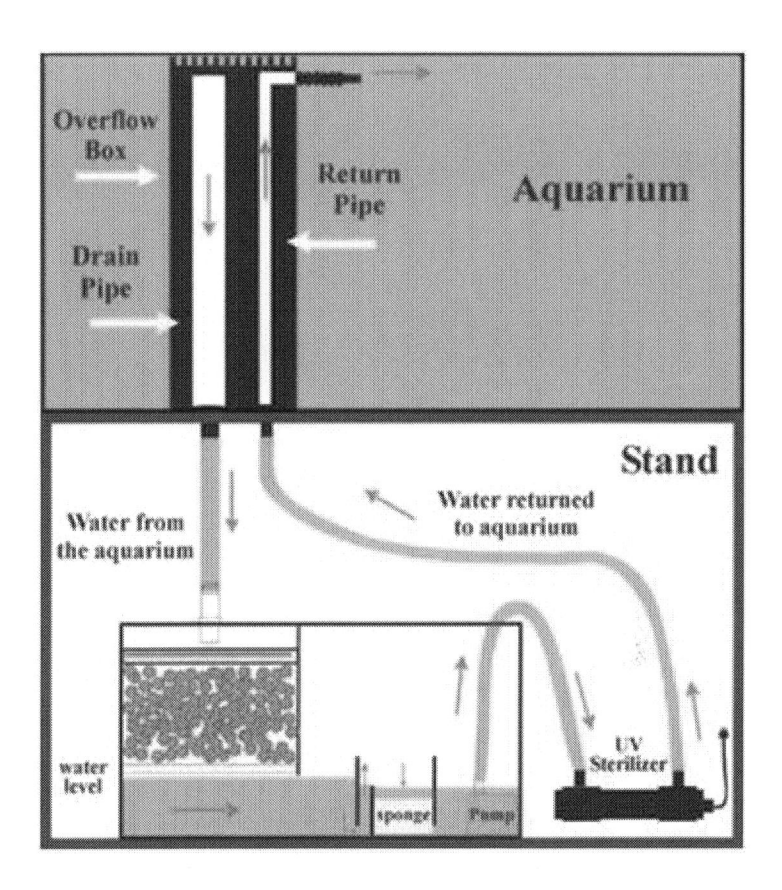

Example of Inline UV sterilizer with wet/dry filter. Same installation with Berlin filter

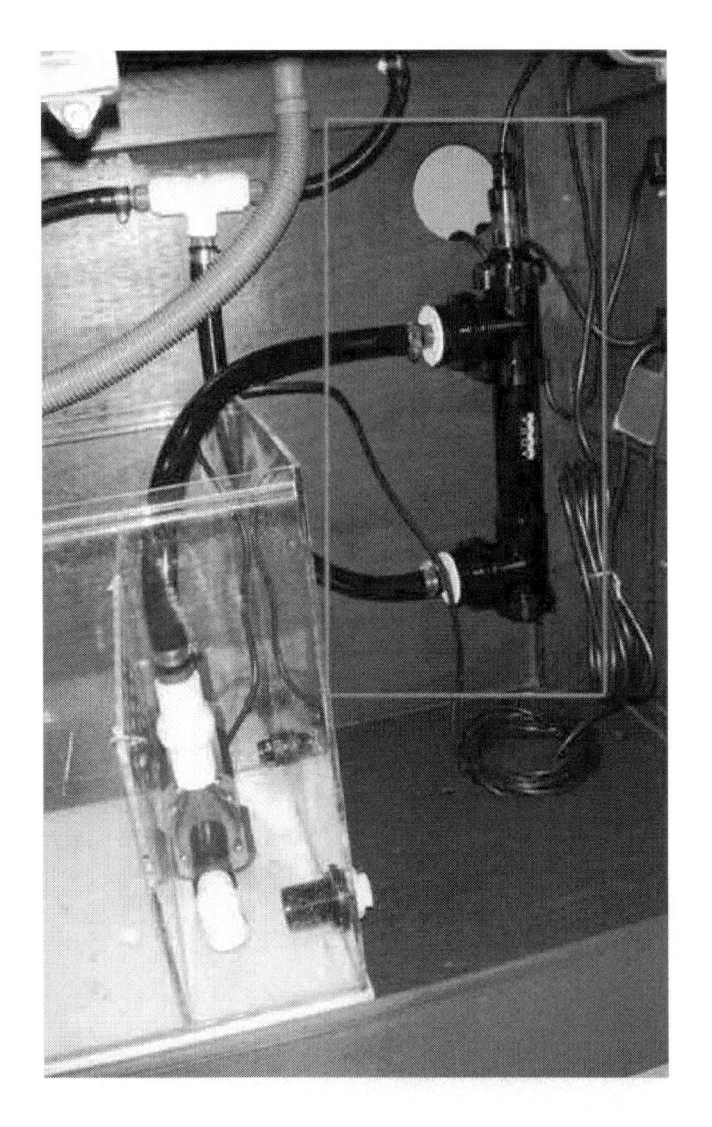

Inline UV sterilizer installed between water pump return and the aquarium

Step 9: Install a Power Strip

Mount power strip(s) inside the cabinet or other protected place. Laying a power strip on the floor behind an aquarium stand is risky as there is then the chance that water could accidentally spill on it. Saltwater and electricity make a bad combination.

Power strips with surge protectors mounted in cabinet

If you have your aquarium sitting on top of a desk or shelf, make sure no water can ever splash on the power outlet or power strip. **Do not plug power outlet strip into wall receptacle at this time.**

Step 10: Install Protein Skimmer

Protein skimmers physically remove dissolved organic compounds and other substances from aquarium water. Assemble the protein skimmer following manufacturer's directions. Place the protein skimmer in the Berlin sump as shown. **DO NOT plug it in at this time.**

Internal protein skimmer in sump

Step 11: Adding live rock

There are many ways to stack live rock to mimic ocean reefs (this was discussed "Choosing and Stacking Live Rock" in Chapter 1). The stacking method we will use is the fore-reef slopes where the rock is stacked high in the back of the aquarium simulating reef walls. This style is aesthetically pleasing and allows the creation of large and/or small caverns for fish to swim through.

Place live rock directly on glass

It is not a good idea to add substrate first because placing live rock on top of the substrate can make structures unstable. Some fish like to burrow and make tunnels and this can cause the rock to tumble. Stacking the rock first and pouring substrate around it creates a more stable structure, less susceptible to being toppled by the antics of burrowing creatures.

Stack rock in a sturdy fashion, yet loosely enough to keep water flowing through it. This will help your water quality. Also leave 1/2 to 3/4 of your substrate open (without rock covering it) to allow healthy water changes to pull out nutrients, organics and waste products from your aquarium.

Note crevices and small caves

Flat rock inserted between two other rocks create a place for fish to perch such as a bicolor blenny

An example of stacked rock - it is not too impressive looking at this point

When stacking live rock, sometimes it will look like a pile of rocks when you finish. As long as you have some caves, crevices and shelves, your rockwork will work fine. If you are not happy with the way your rockwork looks, simply make changes. Since livestock will not be added until The Cycle (see "Water Quality Explained", Chapter 6) is complete, you have time to move a couple of rocks around. Keep in mind when adding and stacking live rock. Some fish grow large and require large caves and openings in the rockwork while others need lots of room to swim.

Completed rock stack in a 210 gallon aquarium

Here is an example of an island live rock stacking; the aquarium will be viewed from the front and back; rocks are stacked in the center of the aquarium without touching the walls

Whichever style of rock formation you choose here are a few rules to follow:
- Try to keep as much of the substrate open as possible.
- Make sure the rocks are stable. Use aquarium epoxy to help stabilize the rock.
- Build caves to allow fish to feel relaxed.
- Use the rocks to hide filter parts (if they are in the aquarium) and to create a natural look.

When stacking live rock you may find that you need a certain shape rock or a certain size rock. Live rock is usually easy to break and shape. A hammer and a chisel will easily break the rock to a smaller size and it is easy to shape a rock to be more stable (wear safety glasses). If your rock stack is still not stable, use reef epoxy. Reef epoxy is available in grey, pink or purple and will bond rocks to each other. Epoxy is also a great way to secure live corals to live rock.

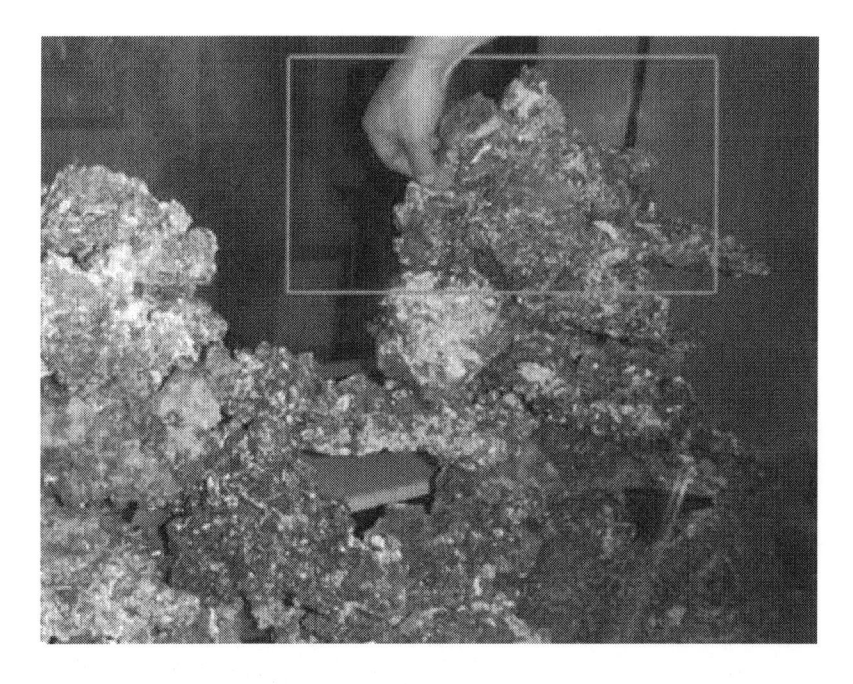

Applying purple-colored epoxy to live rock for support

135

Step 12: Adding Substrate

The substrate you choose should be made of aragonite, a beneficial substrate that slowly dissolves and releases buffers to help keep the pH at an acceptable level for the livestock. Some substrates are clean and require no pre-rinsing.

A popular choice is called live sand. This is coral reef sand either collected live from the ocean or commercially manufactured. Manufactured live sands are readily available and are sands populated with live nitrifying bacteria. The live bacteria should speed up the time an aquarium takes to cycle (ready for livestock). Live sand should not be rinsed.

Another choice of substrate is packaged dry. This substrate may be dusty or dirty simply rinse it in a large bucket, 10 to 15 pounds at a time. Run clean tap water through it, stir and drain it to wash away dust and debris. You may also use a kitchen colander.

Sand is available in many sizes. We will choose a one to two mm size sand since this works for most fish and invertebrates and is easy to vacuum during maintenance.

Some aquarists prefer a deep substrate bed. For our purposes, we will add enough substrate to create a one to two-inch thick layer.

Spreading out the substrate

Pour aragonite into an open spot on the floor of the aquarium. Then spread it evenly on the bottom of the aquarium to a depth of one to two inch thick.

Step 13: The Heater

Set the dial on your submersible heater, to a specific temperature and a thermostat inside the heater will keep the temperature constant. Because there are many heater manufacturers, it is best to follow their specific instructions to set and attach your heater. Place the heater in the sump with the suction cups against the bottom. The suction cups will elevate the heater from the surface of the sump so that water can circulate completely around it. This will permit the heater to work efficiently. **DO NOT plug the heater in to an outlet before adding water.**

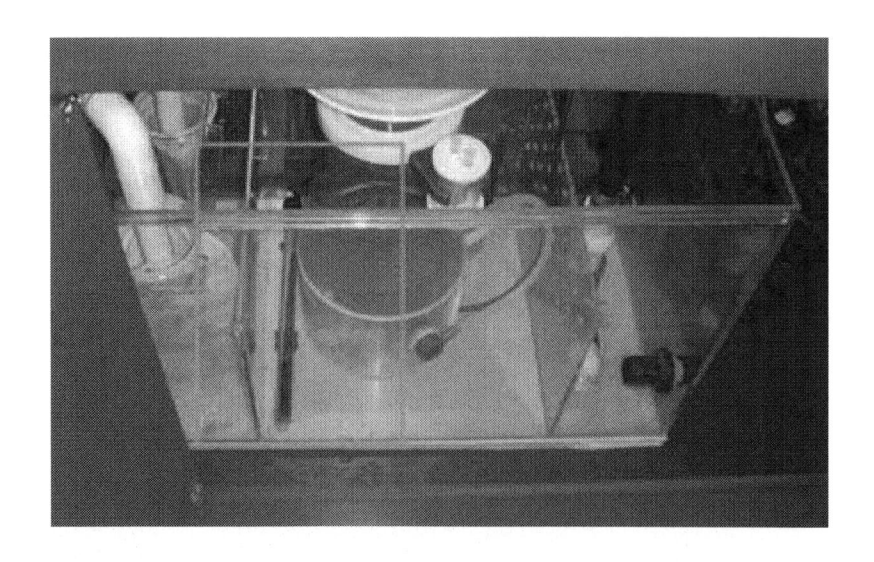

Top view of submersible heater placed in sump

Set the temperature between 80° and 82°F until a biological foundation is established. Once your aquarium is cycled, (see "Water Quality Explained", Chapter 6) set the temperature to between 76° and 78°F.

Step 14: Powerhead

Powerheads help circulate water and increase the current in the aquarium; they keep water flowing through the live rock, reminiscent of the flow of water in the ocean.

Powerheads can be installed on the side or back panes of glass, on either or both sides of the aquarium.

Powerhead (Hydor Koralia) attached with mounting magnet in upper right corner

NOTE: Powerheads need to be cleaned regularly. They can be hidden by live rock just make sure they can be easily removed for cleaning.

Step 15: Adding Water

Since Reverse Osmosis (RO) and Reverse Osmosis with Deionization (RO/DI) water are the best choices, this is what we will use. RO water and RO water mixed with marine salt is often sold in 5-gallon jugs at local fish and pet stores. You can also purchase your own RO filter system (see "Using Purified Water" in Chapter 1 for more information).

If you purchase premixed RO water from the store, the water should be ready to pour into your aquarium. Allow water to become room temperature.

Adding premixed saltwater

CAUTION: When using live rock and live sand substrate you MUST mix the salt and water before adding it to the aquarium. (If you add freshwater directly to your live sand, you can kill the beneficial bacteria in the sand.)

Mixing Your Own Saltwater

If you have your own RO filter system, you must premix your saltwater before adding it to the aquarium. Begin by filling a 5-gallon bucket or larger non-toxic container (preferably with wheels) with RO water. Next, add salt to the water. Follow the instructions on the salt mix, keeping in mind that a general rule is to add approximately one cup of salt to every two gallons of aquarium water.

After mixing salt with the water in the bucket, use a hydrometer to test specific gravity. There are two different types of hydrometers that aquarists use. One is a plastic box with a floating swing-arm and the other looks similar to a floating glass thermometer. Either style will work.

The specific gravity should read between 1.023 and 1.025. If the specific gravity is too low, add more salt. If you add too much salt and the hydrometer reads over the target, remove some of the water and add fresh RO water.

The RO filter system should have removed chlorine and/or chloramines, therefore a water conditioner is not necessary. Test pH and make sure it is between 8.2 and 8.4. If the pH is below 8.2, add a buffering agent to adjust it. (More information about pH can be found in "Water Quality Explained", Chapter 6.)

Pour water slowly onto one of the live rocks close to the bottom of the aquarium. (Since you just spread out the substrate, you do not want to blow it all around.) You can also place a dinner plate in the aquarium temporarily on which to pour the water. Fill the aquarium until the water level is just above the bottom of the aquarium's frame and water begins to flow over the overflow.

At this point you can either continue to add water to the aquarium to fill the Berlin sump in the cabinet or you can pour water directly into the sump until filled to the designated max fill line.

For larger aquariums, carrying water back and forth may take too much time and energy. You may want to purchase a new thirty-five to forty-five gallon trashcan or other non-toxic, plastic container (with wheels). Whichever size container you choose it should **only** be used for your aquarium. Once the salt is mixed in the container, roll it over to the aquarium. The premixed saltwater can either be bucketed into the aquarium or a water pump with flexible tubing attached can be used to pump the water into the aquarium.

Step 16: Setting Up a Refugium (recommended option)

If you chose to use a refugium get one which is built in to a Berlin sump. A built-in refugium is a compartment in a Berlin sump which houses mud or sand and algae. The walls of the compartment are made to allow water to pass through and return to the display aquarium. These walls also slow water flow to assist with macro algae feeding.

The size of the refugium needed depends on the bio-load of the display aquarium. A larger refugium is necessary for a heavily stocked aquarium; smaller refugium may be used for a lightly stocked aquarium.

Refugiums are easy to setup just add mud and/or an oolithic (sugar size) aragonite sand to a depth of up to six inches and macro algae.

Berlin sump with refugium compartment with oolithic sand

Place a light over the refugium to help grow macro algae. The bulb should be 5,000 to 6,500 Kelvin for optimum plant growth. Choose a light fixture that produces at least four watts per gallon of water in the refugium (for those less than 16 inches deep).

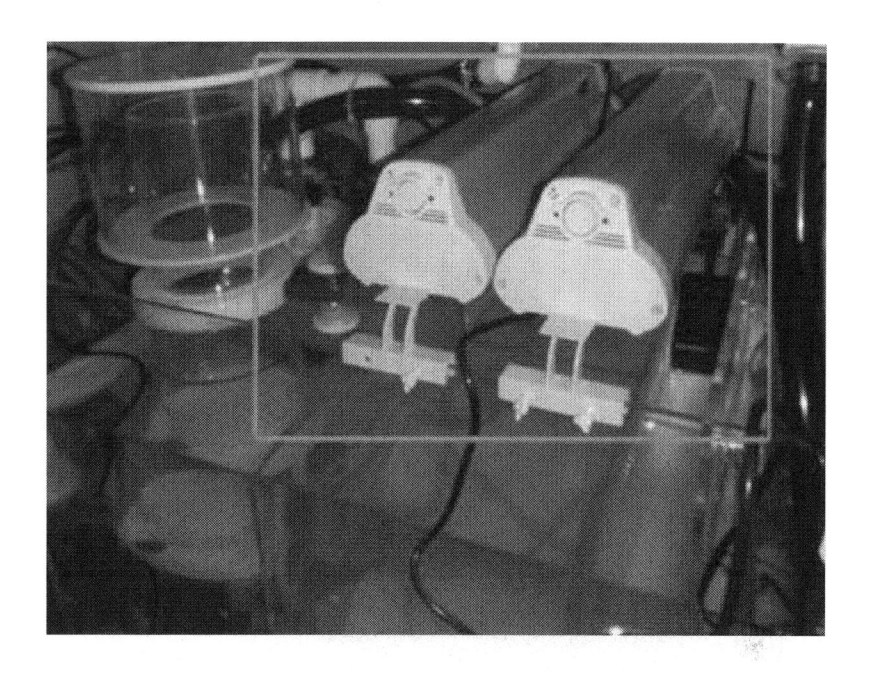

Two T5 strip lights mounted above refugium

TIP: Set the refugium light to turn on when the aquarium light turns off. For more information see "Refugium" in Chapter 1.

Macro algae can be added to refugium 24 hours after aquarium is setup or you can wait until the aquarium has "cycled". Chaetomorpha, Ulva (Sea Lettuce), halimeda (red seaweed) and Gracilaria (red seaweed) are macro algae that do well in refugiums.

Step 17: Starting the Equipment

It is time to plug in the water pump, which returns water to the aquarium into an electrical outlet. The water should start leaving the sump and flow into the aquarium. Soon water will flow back down into the sump over the overflow box. Add water to the sump if need to until it reaches the fill line on the side of the Berlin sump.

Plug in to an electrical outlet the water pump on the protein skimmer and follow manufacturer's directions to properly adjust your protein skimmer.

Install a Thermometer

Attach a hanging thermometer to the aquarium or inside the Berlin sump. Do not put a thermometer in the return pump compartment if you do not have a prefilter on the pump.

Keep a thermometer in the aquarium or sump as it allows you to ensure the heater works properly and, during the warm months, it helps you keep tabs that the aquarium is not getting too hot.

> *NOTE: A thermometer is also necessary for water changes. When you change aquarium water, you want to make sure the new water is within two degrees of the temperature of the water in your aquarium.*

Plug in the Heater

Once the water is in the sump, wait ten to fifteen minutes before plugging in the heater to allow the temperature of the heater's glass tube to acclimate to the temperature of the water. This will prevent the glass tube from cracking due to a rapid change in temperature.

> *SAFETY TIP: Make sure any electrical wires leading from your filter, heater, and lights to an electrical outlet have drip loops. If a drop of water travels down your cord it will drip at the bottom of the loop before it enters your electrical socket. Electrical cords, when plugged into the electrical outlet, must loop below the outlet.*

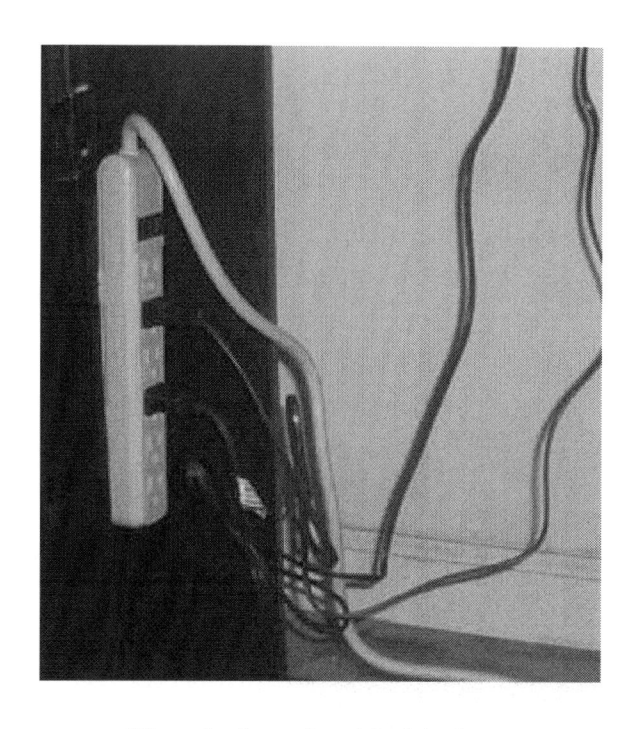

Electrical cords with drip loop

Step 18: Placing the Glass tops, Light and Canopy

Place the hood or glass tops on the aquarium, set the strip light on the glass tops, plug it in and turn on the light.

Aquarium with glass tops and 48" strip light

The lights can also be mounted directly in a canopy. If glass tops are not used the inside of a wooden canopy must be sealed to make it water proof.

If you are using un-cured live rock, the lights should remain off until rock has cycled. If you are using cured live rock, you can have your lights on for a couple of hours a day. Lots of light can cause unwanted algae growing in your aquarium. Reducing the light to a few hours a day will help control algae growth. When water has cycled and livestock has been added, than the lights can run for 6 to 10 hours a day.

Step 19: The Final Step

Put a canopy (if you have one) on the aquarium. The saltwater aquarium is completely setup; stand back and enjoy your creation!

Island stacked saltwater aquarium completely assembled; water will be crystal clear within 24 hours

120 Gallon aquarium with live rock

At this point, your aquarium is completely setup. Now is the perfect time to learn a about water quality and testing equipment.

Once the live rock has cycled (discussed in "Water Quality Explained", Chapter 6), you are ready to do a partial water change and add some livestock.

Chapter 5

How to Assemble a Drilled Aquarium with Artificial Decorations

There are only a few differences between setting up an aquarium with live rock and setting one up using only artificial decorations. If you are setting up an aquarium with artificial decorations, follow the live rock setup instructions in Chapter 4 with the exception of these few changes:

Step 6 gives instruction on installing a Berlin Filter. Instead of using a Berlin filter use wet/dry filter which contains biological filter media.

Wet/dry filter with blue bio media

Live rock has tons of surface area on which beneficial bacteria can grow and colonize. Artificial decorations are normally removed and cleaned periodically, killing and removing beneficial bacteria. Even if the decorations are not removed and cleaned they normally cannot provide enough surface area to colonize sufficient beneficial bacteria to handle the fish bio load. Installation of a wet/dry filter is similar to that of a Berlin filter; water drains from the aquarium into the wet/dry filter and is returned to the aquarium through tubes.

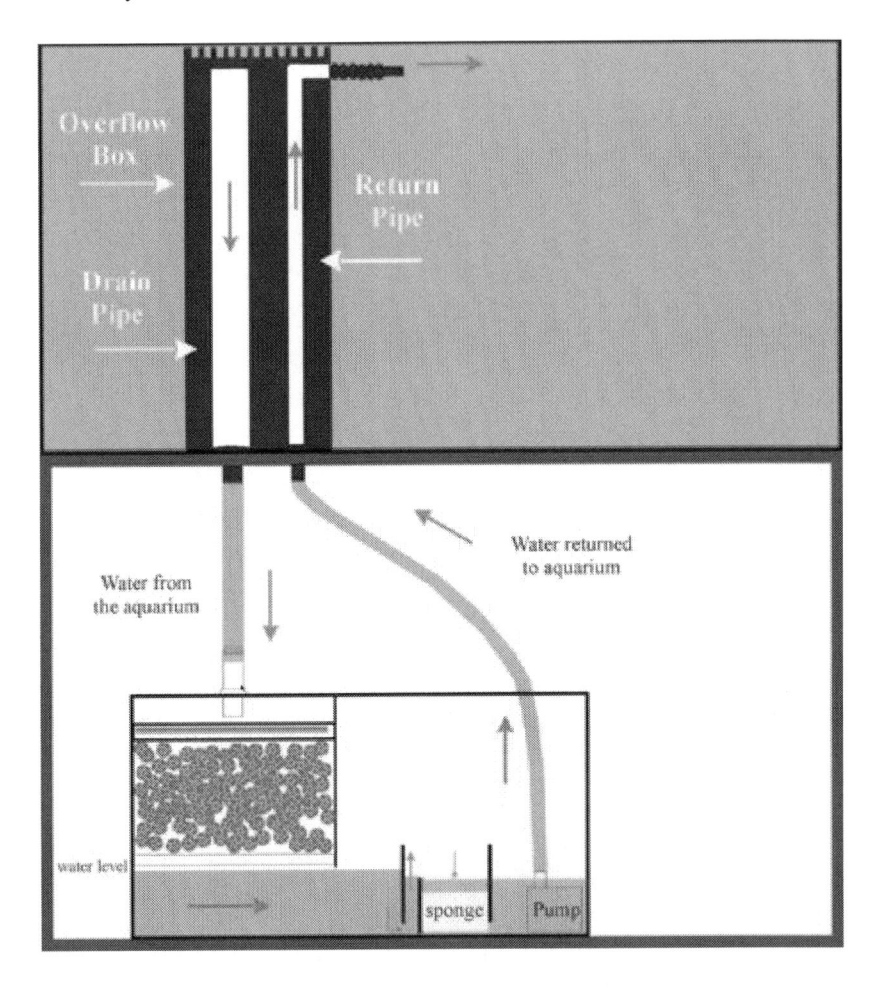

Diagram with wet/dry filter installation

Step 11 walks you through the process of adding and stacking live rock. Instead of adding live rock, rinse off decorations in plain water and place them in your desired locations. There are no hard, fast rules for decoration placement; we are all individuals and have our own tastes so have fun and decorate until you are happy with the outcome. Be aware that fish need to feel safe as if they are in their natural environment and they need hiding places to feel secure. Too few decorations is to your fish as a room with sparse furniture is to most people.

Saltwater aquarium with artificial decorations manufactured by Living Color

Here are a few decorating suggestions to help you get started:

First, place the largest pieces of artificial coral a little towards the back of the aquarium. If you have three large pieces of coral decorations you can place them in a V shape such that the right and left pieces are placed more to the back and the one in the center is placed toward the middle of the aquarium.

Place smaller pieces of coral randomly around your aquarium.

It is a good idea to place artificial plants close to the coral to leave some room for fish to swim. If you have plants that are the same type but different heights, place them near each other to give a natural effect of plants growing.

Use the tallest plants near the back or sides of the aquarium. Tall plants will stand out and can be placed near structures and caves. Alternatively, put a large plant alone in the center of your tank and add smaller plants around it. Use medium sized plants in front of larger plants to provide a feeling of different levels, to add color and depth, and to enlarge the bigger plant to make it look fuller.

Finally, yet importantly, place your short plants. These plants are the final pieces to your masterpiece. Use them as abstract pieces for color or size and place them between, in front of, or just around other decorations in your aquarium. The best part about decorating is that it is fun and should you want to make changes, you can do so easily.

Step 12 provides instructions on adding substrate to the aquarium. Follow the instructions for adding substrate, except add it **before** adding plants and decorations.

Make these few changes to the live rock setup instructions in Chapter 4 for a beautiful aquarium.
Now is the perfect time to learn about water quality.

Chapter 6

Water Quality Explained

Good water quality is essential to keeping fish healthy and alive for years.

Why test water?

Our goal is to create an environment in which our saltwater fish and invertebrates will thrive. The only way to determine if the quality of the aquarium water is ideal is to test it.

What needs to be tested?

The basic tests to perform regularly on aquarium water are pH, ammonia, nitrite, nitrate, calcium and KH and specific gravity.

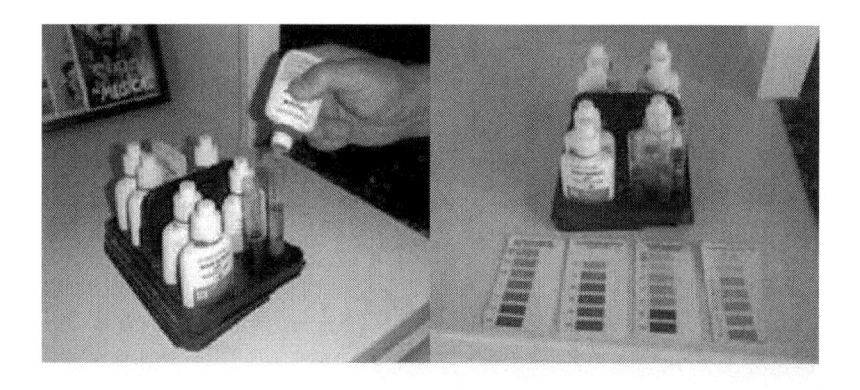

The majority of aquarium test kits are easy to use

Let us look at why these tests are necessary.

pH

A simple understanding of pH is helpful to keep your fish healthy. The term pH refers to how acidic or basic a substance is. The pH scale ranges from 0 to 14; 7 is neutral. A pH reading lower than 7 indicates an acid, a reading higher than 7 indicates a base.

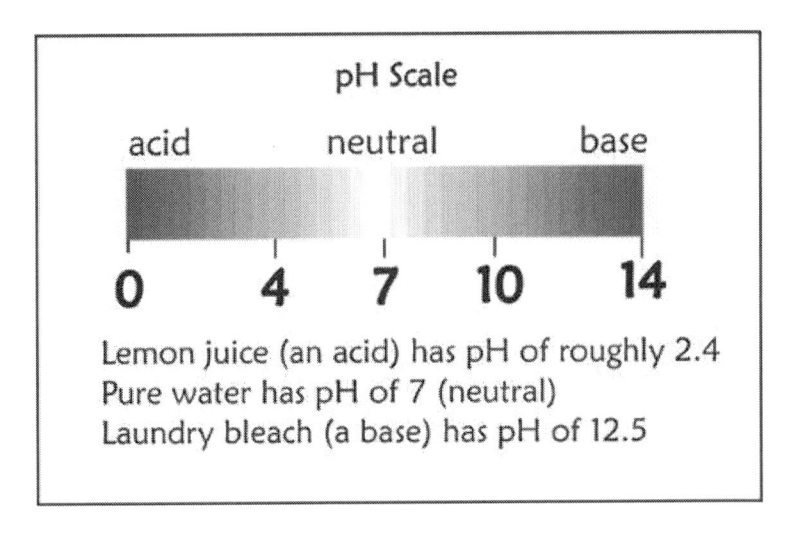

pH Scale

acid   neutral   base

0   4   7   10   14

Lemon juice (an acid) has pH of roughly 2.4
Pure water has pH of 7 (neutral)
Laundry bleach (a base) has pH of 12.5

pH scale, saltwater fish need a high pH compared to most freshwater fish

For saltwater fish, the optimal pH level is 8.0 to 8.4.

Test aquarium water and adjust pH, if necessary, before adding fish. Most fish prefer gradual changes in pH but you can adjust an unpopulated aquarium very quickly. Should a change in pH be necessary, add a buffering agent. There are many buffering agents on the market; choose one and follow directions carefully. Once pH is at the appropriate level, you are ready to add fish.

Other kits test ammonia, nitrite and nitrate are important after fish have been in the aquarium for a while. They are helpful in determining how your tank is cycling. These test kits measure compounds that are harmful to the fish.

For the first few weeks, a new aquarium is a stressful environment for fish. Knowing this can be a key to successfully selecting your first fish.

Specific Gravity

There are two different types of hydrometers used to test specific gravity, which measure the salt levels in a reef aquarium. One is a plastic box with a floating swing-arm and the other looks similar to a floating glass thermometer. Either style will work. Follow the manufacturers' directions and test your specific gravity.

Specific gravity should read between 1.020 and 1.025. If it is too low, add more salt. If you add too much salt and the hydrometer reads over the target, remove some of the water and add fresh water.

NOTE: The next section, The Nitrogen Cycle, is divided into two parts: setting up and aquarium using live rock and setting up an aquarium using artificial decorations. If you are setting up your aquarium with live rock, keep reading. To set up an aquarium with artificial decorations, skip to "The Nitrogen Cycle - Aquarium Setup with Artificial Decorations".

The Nitrogen Cycle - Aquarium with Live Rock

The Nitrogen Cycle

Once live rock is assembled and sand added to your aquarium, your tank will begin a process called The Nitrogen Cycle (we will just call it The Cycle for short). The Cycle does not begin until there are waste products from live rock present in the water. This waste product is produced from once live, now deceased and decaying organisms on live rock. Their deaths are caused by shipping, handling and even just moving the rock from one aquarium to another.

As live rock is prepared for transport, shippers wrap it in newspaper to preserve the moisture. Even so, much of the sea life on the rock quickly begins to dry out. When packed in shipping boxes, the rocks rub against each other killing even more sea life in those spots.

Deceased life, whether animal, bacteria or plant, decays, producing waste that is toxic to fish. This waste product begins in the form of ammonia and, if left unchecked, the fish, corals and invertebrates would simply die.

Thankfully, nature has a relatively simple and natural system that will keep our animals alive. While harmful to livestock, ammonia provides food to bacteria, called nitrosomonas, which are very beneficial in an aquarium. These bacteria break down ammonia into something called nitrite.

Nitrite is also harmful to livestock, but as luck would have it, yet another naturally occurring bacteria, nitrospira, uses harmful nitrite and gives off a byproduct called nitrate.

Nitrate is less toxic than either ammonia or nitrite.

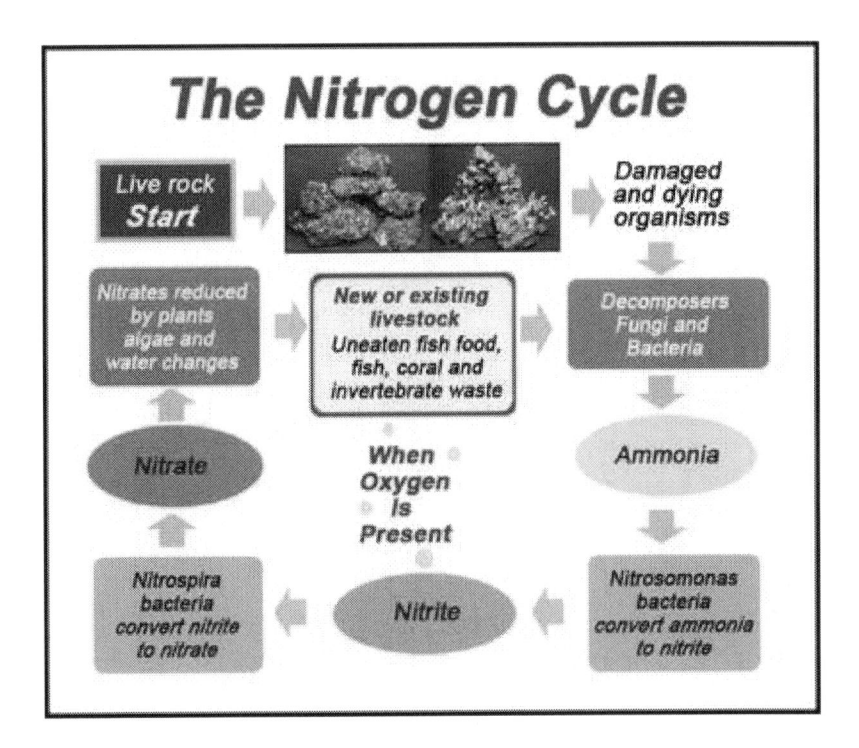

The Nitrogen Cycle

- Live rock **Start** → Damaged and dying organisms
- Damaged and dying organisms → Decomposers Fungi and Bacteria
- Decomposers Fungi and Bacteria → Ammonia
- Ammonia → Nitrosomonas bacteria convert ammonia to nitrite
- Nitrosomonas bacteria convert ammonia to nitrite → Nitrite
- Nitrite → Nitrospira bacteria convert nitrite to nitrate
- Nitrospira bacteria convert nitrite to nitrate → Nitrate
- Nitrate → Nitrates reduced by plants, algae and water changes
- Nitrates reduced by plants, algae and water changes → New or existing livestock, Uneaten fish food, fish, coral and invertebrate waste

When Oxygen Is Present

Flowchart of The Nitrogen Cycle

It takes two to six weeks for beneficial bacteria to become established when the aquarium water is 80°F. This process may take longer at lower temperatures. Because high levels of ammonia and nitrite are stressful to livestock, no animals should be introduced once

The Cycle begins. After The Cycle finishes (when both ammonia and nitrite levels are zero), a partial water change is recommended (see "How to Care for Your Aquarium", Chapter 11) and now the livestock can then be added.

A protein skimmer is very beneficial at removing a lot of the organic waste before it is broken down into ammonia.

Several bacteria starters are on the market today that can shorten cycling time. These products contain live cultures of beneficial bacteria; add them directly to aquarium water at the same time you add live rock to jump-start the bacteria that occur naturally.

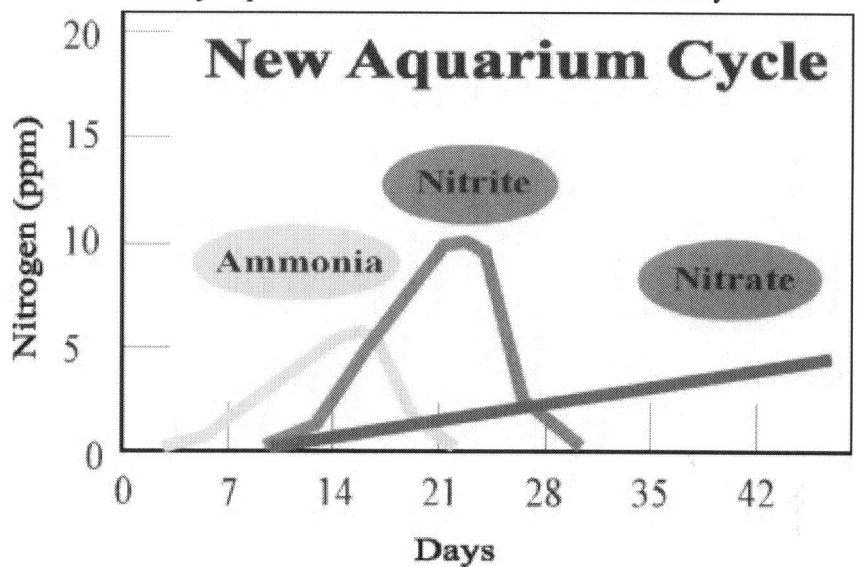

New Aquarium Cycle

This chart illustrates the Nitrogen Cycle Process. Actual levels of ammonia, nitrite and nitrate may vary. Many factors determine these levels: whether the live rock is cured or uncured, if a protein skimmer is used, the temperature of the water and how quickly beneficial bacteria become established.

You now see why test kits are helpful in determining where the levels are during The Cycle. Ammonia and nitrite test kits will determine harmful compound levels so that we know when the aquarium is ready for livestock. You can see that ammonia and nitrite are controlled biologically by beneficial bacteria and with a protein skimmer. It can also be reduced by water changes (see "How to Care for Your Aquarium", Chapter 11). Normally we do not change water when cycling with cured live rock.

Once beneficial bacteria are established, it is safe to add fish, corals or inverts a few at a time to allow "good" bacteria to keep up with the increase of waste. If too much livestock is added, there may be toxic spikes in ammonia or nitrite.

The Nitrogen Cycle - Aquarium Setup with Artificial Decorations

The Nitrogen Cycle

Having a basic understanding of The Nitrogen Cycle is critical to keep fish healthy and thriving. Once you add fish to your aquarium, your tank will begin a process called The Nitrogen Cycle (we will just call it The Cycle for short). The Cycle does not begin until there are waste products (from your fish or live rock) present in the water. Soon after you add fish to your aquarium and feed them, fish begin to create waste. There is not a specific area designated for fish to excrete feces, so fish waste (ammonia) just remains in the water. Ammonia is toxic to your fish, and, if left in this water with no filter, the fish would simply die.

As discussed previously, we can thankfully work with nature and create a system that will keep our fish alive! We mimic as closely as possible the natural habitats of fish by filtering the water in our aquariums and by changing water on occasion. We use our knowledge of The Cycle to our advantage.

The process is relatively simple. While harmful to fish, ammonia provides food to bacteria, called nitrosomonas, which are very beneficial in an aquarium. These bacteria break down ammonia into something called nitrite.

Nitrite is also harmful to fish, but other naturally occurring bacteria, nitrospira, use harmful nitrite and give off a byproduct called nitrate.

Nitrate is less toxic to fish than either ammonia or nitrite and will either be utilized by plant life or removed with simple water changes.

The Nitrogen Cycle

fish respiration
fish waste
uneaten fish food

fish food Start

Decomposers Fungi and Bacteria

uneaten fish food decaying fish and plants

Nitrates reduced by plants, algaes and water changes

Ammonia

When Oxygen is Present

Nitrate

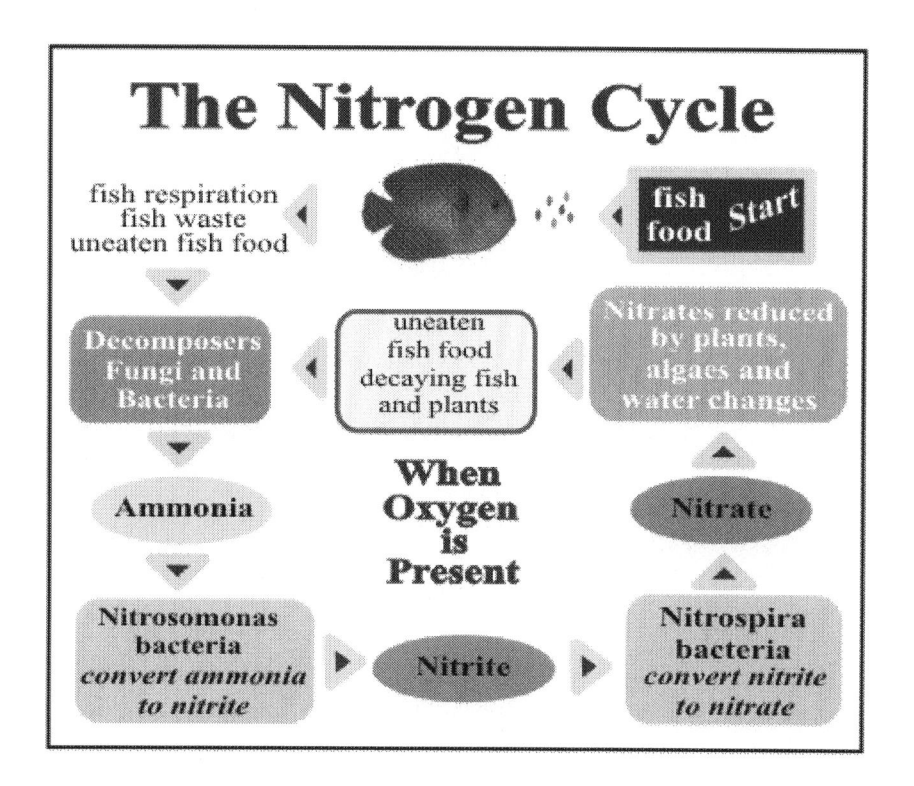

Nitrosomonas bacteria *convert ammonia to nitrite*

Nitrite

Nitrospira bacteria *convert nitrite to nitrate*

It takes 4 to 6 weeks for beneficial bacteria to become established when the aquarium water is 80°F. This process may take longer at lower temperatures. Because high levels of ammonia and nitrite are stressful to fish, no additional fish should be introduced once The Cycle begins; it is wise to refrain from changing water during this time, except in extreme instances. After The Cycle finishes (when both ammonia and nitrite levels are zero), a water change is recommended and more fish can then be added.

Several bacteria starters are on the market today that can shorten cycling time. These products contain live cultures of beneficial bacteria; add them directly to aquarium water at the same time you add fish or live rock to jump-start the bacteria that occur naturally.

New Aquarium Cycle

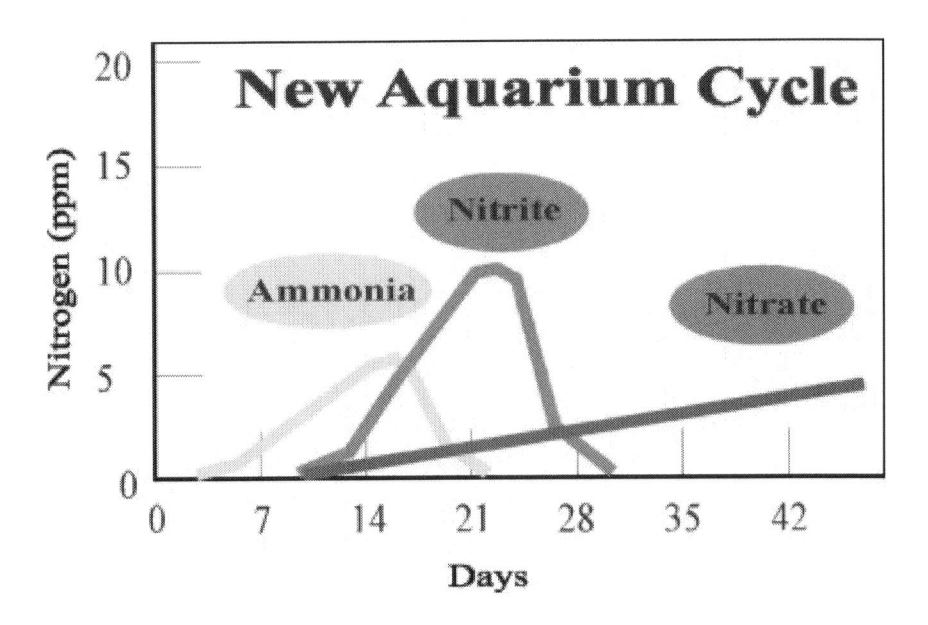

(chart showing Nitrogen (ppm) vs Days, with Ammonia, Nitrite, and Nitrate curves over 0–42 days)

This chart illustrates the Nitrogen Cycle Process. Actual levels of ammonia, nitrite and nitrate may vary. There are many factors that determine these levels such as the number and size of fish, how often and how much they are fed, temperature and how fast beneficial bacteria become established.

Nitrate

As we just discussed, the byproduct of the Nitrogen Cycle is nitrates. Nitrates build up slowly over time. Fish can tolerate a high level of nitrates but even a low level of nitrate can be harmful to corals and invertebrates. To keep this level in check, use a nitrate test kit. If the results read less than 10 ppm, then all is well. If Nitrate level needs to be reduced, accomplish this through water changes (with low or zero nitrate replacement water), reduce the amount of food you are feeding your fish, remove any dead fish, inverts or decaying plant matter, replace nitrate-removing media to just name a few.

NOTE: Micro and macro algae (plants) use nitrates as a food source.

FREE BONUS: To get your FREE Water Testing Tracking Form, go to http://9nl.be/Freebonuses

Once our water is ideal we can get to the fun part: adding livestock. Let us begin with saltwater fish.

Chapter 7

How to Choose Fish for a Saltwater Aquarium

Add fish when you are certain the filter is running, specific gravity is between 1.020 and 1.0254, pH is between 8.0 and 8.4 and the heater is working. Water should be clear. Do not be concerned if you see some air bubbles on the sides of the aquarium and decorations, they are harmless. (Wipe bubbles from the glass with an aquarium sponge and shake bubbles from artificial plants if you desire. They will go away on their own and there is no need for all the bubbles to be gone before adding fish.)

If you are setting up your aquarium with live rock, The Cycle must be complete before fish can be added. The Cycle begins naturally as deceased and decaying organism in live rock are the foods required to grow beneficial bacteria. Fish and invertebrates can be introduced as soon as the beneficial bacteria have reduced the ammonia and nitrite levels to zero when tested. This process generally takes one to four weeks depending on whether cured or uncured rock was used.

If you are setting up your aquarium using artificial decorations it makes sense to wait 24 hours before adding fish just to be certain that the heater and filter are working properly. Remember, the tank will only begin cycling once fish are added. Beneficial bacteria need a food source and fish waste supplies this food source.

Using fish to Cycle your aquarium is stressful on them; therefore, you will want to choose hardy fish in the beginning. In the fish industry many hardy fish are referred to as starter fish. Starter fish, like all fish, provide waste products that feed beneficial bacteria; they are generally strong enough to withstand high ammonia and nitrite levels. Starter fish include but are not limited to damselfish, clownfish and groupers (aggressive).

To reduce the stress on fish going through The Cycle and to shorten the span of this cycle, it is wise to add a bacteria starter. Bacteria starters contain live cultures of beneficial bacteria; add them directly to aquarium water at the same time you add fish or live rock to jump-start the bacteria that occur naturally.

Throughout the following pages, you will see many fish from which to choose. (Once your aquarium has finished cycling, it will be safe to add some of these fish.) You will learn about the diets of many species. The fish will be broken down into categories: carnivores, herbivores and omnivores. Carnivorous fish eat meat; herbivores eat algae, seaweed and vegetables; omnivores eat both meat and vegetables.

Because we are talking about general categories there may be individuals in a species such that one is a carnivore and another is an omnivore. For example, the Yellow Watchman Goby is a meat eater while the Court Jester Goby eats meat and filamentous algae.

If you plan to add invertebrates like snails, shrimp and crabs to your aquarium there are many meat-eating fish which consider them food. Have no worries, there is a large array of fish that will cohabitate well with most invertebrates. The key is obviously to choose your fish wisely so they all get along.

Common Names to Scientific Names

You will find that many fish have multiple names, common names and scientific names. Some fish even have multiple common names. The Pacific Blue Tang, for example, is also called Hippo Tang, Regal Tang and Yellow Tail Tang. The scientific name of the Pacific Blue Tang is Paracanthurus hepatus.

Angelfish - Dwarf

Coral Beauty Angelfish (*Centropyge bispinosa*), Flame Angelfish (*Centropyge loriculus*), Flameback Angelfish (African) (*Centropyge acanthops*), Pygmy (Cherub) Angelfish (*Centropyge argi*), Red Stripe Angelfish (*Centropyge eibli*), Rusty Angelfish (Centropyge ferrugata) and Venustus Angelfish (*Sumireyakko venustus*)

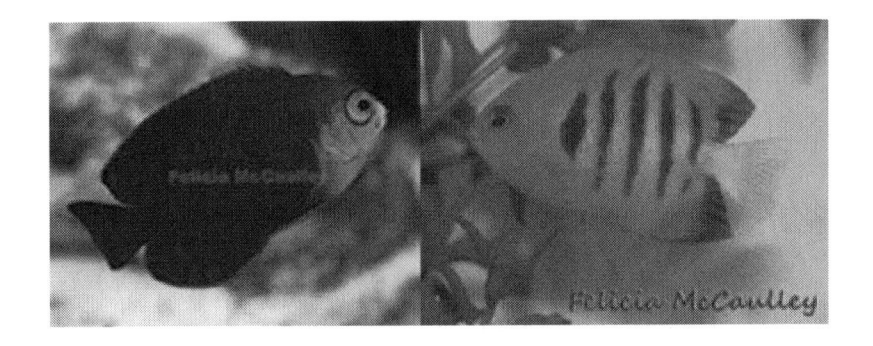

Pygmy and Flame Angelfish

Coral Beauty and African Pygmy Angelfish

    Most Dwarf Angelfish have bright vivid colors and live long, beautiful lives in established aquariums. Angelfish can be easily distinguished from other species by a sharp spine located at the lower front of the gill cover; this is their weapon for protection or to attack other fish.

    Depending on the species, dwarf Angelfish grow to three to six inches in length. These fish are generally compatible with other species like tangs, Gobies, Wrasses, etc, but are usually aggressive towards each other. Dwarf angels tend to be territorial, and for this reason it is best to keep only one in a small aquarium. In larger aquariums, dwarf Angelfish of different sizes can live together. Try to add juvenile Angelfish at the same time to your aquarium so that they grow and change together.

To feel secure, Angelfish like lots of caves and places to hide.

Angelfish spend most of their day picking or nipping at algae and detritus on sand, rocks, corals, aquarium glass, etc. Dwarf angels are omnivorous and within a short time after being added to an aquarium will eat almost any food offered. Feed them a variety of foods to create a balanced diet of meats and algae.

If you are planning on keeping corals and clams then there is a downside to some of the dwarf angelfish. They will eat (nip) mucous produced by the corals and clams, rather than the flesh itself. If corals are healthy this nipping may not be a problem, but nipping may cause certain corals to stay retracted. If a coral remains retracted, and no longer opens, part of, or even the entire coral may die. Sometimes just moving a coral to a different location will cause the angel to leave it alone. Tridacna clams can also be harassed to death by a persistent nibbler. Retracting its fleshy mantle tissue repeatedly can exhaust a clam and even lead to death.

This said, a dwarf Angelfish makes a beautiful addition to a saltwater aquarium and they generally do well in mini reef. Choose your Angelfish wisely, keeping in mind that once a fish is added to an aquarium with live rock they can be very difficult to remove.

CAUTION: Dwarf Angels have a sharp spine located at the lower front of the gill cover which can get caught in a fish net. To transport, herd these little fish into a plastic container.

Angelfish - Large

Annularis Angelfish (Pomacanthus annularis), Bellus Angelfish (*Genicanthus bellus*), Blue Angelfish (Holacanthus bermudensis), Blue Girdled Angelfish (Pomacanthus navarchus), Blueface Angelfish (Pomacanthus xanthometopon), Emperor Angelfish (Pomacanthus imperator), Lamarck's Angelfish (*Genicanthus lamarck*), Japanese Swallowtail Angelfish (*Genicanthus melanospilos*), Koran Angelfish (Pomacanthus semicirculatus), Passer Angelfish (Holacanthus passer), Queen Angelfish (Holacanthus ciliaris) and Watanabei Angelfish (*Genicanthus watanabei*)

Emperor and Majestic Angelfish (both showing adult coloration)

Japanese Swallowtail (Female) and Bellus Angelfish (Female)

Large Angelfish include some of the most majestic, beautiful fish in the world, and are often the most prized possessions for hobbyists. Many of these fish have dazzling bold colors with striking patterns and adapt well to captivity. Large Angelfish can live over twenty years in an aquarium as long as they are kept in a suitable size aquarium, are mixed with compatible fish and are fed a diet which meets their specific requirements.

If you are looking for large reef-safe Angelfish your best choices can be found under the genus Genicanthus, also known as Swallowtail angels. Genicanthus Angelfish will typically mix safely with corals, shrimp, crabs and snails, etc. Rarely do these Angelfish feed on coral polyps, especially if kept well-nourished. Another great attribute of Genicanthus angels is that it is easy to distinguish the males from the females. This means that in a large aquarium you can add a pair of

Angelfish. With some species, you can actually add a school of them! If your reef is small, a lone male or female will do well.

A little research goes far in choosing a large Angel since even in large home aquariums many of these fish can grow well over nine inches long. Most are compatible with species such as large Clownfish, Groupers, Tangs, Triggerfish and Wrasses. Typically it is best to keep one large Angelfish per aquarium with the exception of the above mentioned Genicanthus species.

Just like Dwarf angels, large Angelfish have a sharp spine located on the lower front of the gill cover. They use this spine to protect themselves and to attack other fish. Keep your Angelfish happy and secure by creating plenty of caves and places for it/them to hide.

One of the keys to keeping Angelfish healthy is to research their diet requirements and feed them several times each day. In general, feed them a variety of foods since they are omnivorous and some species require sponge in their diet. A typical Angelfish diets should include spirulina, marine algae, chopped shrimp, clams, squid, and mysis shrimp, as well as prepared enriched frozen foods.

CAUTION: Angels have a sharp spine located at the lower front of the gill cover which can get caught in a fish net. To transport, herd these fish into a plastic container or use a net with very fine mesh.

Basslet

Black Cap Basslet (Gramma melacara), Chalk Bass (*Serranus tortugarum*), Royal Gramma Basslet (*Gramma loreto*), Harlequin Basslet (Serranus tigrinus), Lantern Basslet (Serranus baldwini), Swalesi Basslet (*Liopropoma swalesi*) and Swissguard Basslet (*Liopropoma rubre*)

Royal Gramma and Chalk Bass

Basslets are a popular fish since they stay small, are very hardy, are easy to care for and most are inexpensive (compared to many saltwater fish). Several species of Basslets have bright colors. Royal Grammas, for instance, are a magnificent purple on the front part of their body with a brilliant yellow back portion.

Most Basslets remain small, growing to only about two to three inches long. For protection in the wild, Basslets live in and around rocky areas. In the home aquarium, make sure you have lots of caves and hiding places so they will feel secure.

Since many Basslets are territorial they are best when kept only one per aquarium. Chalk Basslets are an exception to this rule as they are *not* territorial. If your aquarium is large and you add several at the same time, they should do well together.

Basslets are carnivores, require a high protein diet, and will readily eat almost any frozen fish food. They are safe with corals but may eat small ornamental crustaceans; small shrimp, snails and crabs might be at risk to these otherwise adorable fish.

Blennies

Barnacle Blenny (*Acanthemblemaria macrospilus*), Bicolor Blenny (*Ecsenius bicolor*), Black Combtooth Blenny (*Ecsenius namiyei*), Canary Blenny (*Meiacanthus oualanensis*), Black Sailfin Blenny (*Atrosalarias fuscus*), Ember Blenny (*Cirripectes stigmaticus*), Forktail Blenny (*Meiacanthus atrodorsalis*), Green Canary Blenny (*Meiacanthus tongaensis*), Harptail Blenny

(*Meiacanthus mossambicus*), Horseface Blenny (*Ophioblennius atlanticus*), Midas Blenny (*Ecsenius midas*), Lawnmower Blenny (*Salarias fasciatus*), Starry Blenny (*Salarias ramosus*) and Striped Blenny (*Meiacanthus grammistes*)

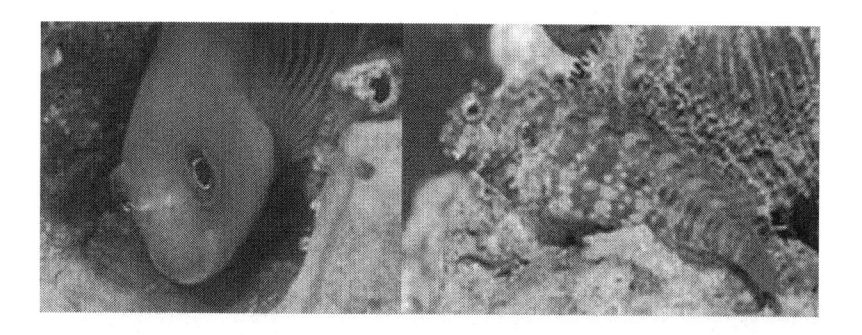

Bicolor and Lawnmower Blenny

Blennies are a large diverse family with most being hardy, easy to care for and do well in an aquarium. Only a relatively few of the blennies species listed above are reef safe.

Blennies are entertaining and fun to watch. Most Blennies will prop themselves up on their pectoral fins and watch everything that goes on around them. Most Blennies will spend much time near or on the bottom of the aquarium. Blennies are very curious and nervous; if startled they quickly dart to safety in a rock, crevice or cave.

There are a few brilliant yellow Blennies, but the majority of species are plain, dull colors. Many will grow to about three inches long while others can grow over six inches in length. Blennies are territorial towards members of their own species so it is ideal to keep just one of any particular species in an aquarium.

Some Blennies are herbivores, others carnivores, and still others are omnivorous. Many will graze on microalgae growing on the rocks and sand. Unfortunately, some Blennies, such as bicolor, algae or lawnmower and horse face Blennies may nip at stony coral polyps and clam mantles. Others, like Barnacle Blennies, are totally reef safe. Barnacle Blennies, as the name might imply, are adorable miniature fish whose maximum length of two inches makes it easy for them to slide into tiny holes in the live rock and call them home. At feeding time, a barnacle blenny darts out of its hole at lightning speed, grabs a piece of food and darts back in to its home. If you blink, you will miss it!

Since Blennies are very diverse, you need to research your favorite blenny before going out and buying it.

Cardinalfish

Five-Lined Cardinalfish (*Cheilodipterus quinquelineatus*), Flame Cardinal (*Apogon spp.*), Banggai Cardinalfish (*Pterapogon kauderni*), Longspine Cardinalfish (*Zoramia leptacantha*), Orbic Cardinalfish (*Sphaeramia orbicularis*), Pajama Cardinalfish (*Sphaeramia nematoptera*) and Yellowstriped Cardinalfish (*Ostorhinchus cyanosoma*)

Banggai and Pajama Cardinalfish

Cardinalfish are yet another popular saltwater fish that are easy to care for. Cardinalfish are easy to distinguish by the distinctive two separate dorsal fins on their backs. Their large eyes are common in nocturnal fish. Since Cardinalfish are nocturnal you may see them spending the day in caves and other shaded areas in your aquarium and find them more active at night. As a group they stay small; most species are less than four inches long.

Peaceful towards their tank mates, many species of Cardinalfish such as Longspine Cardinalfish do well in schools, while others, like Flame Cardinal, prefer to be in pairs.

Cardinalfish are carnivores and most will readily eat a varied diet.

Banggai, Pajama and Longspine Cardinalfish are bred in captivity. An odd fact about Cardinalfish is that a male will hold fertilized eggs in his mouth for protection. In about a week the eggs will hatch. It is possible for baby Cardinalfish to survive in hobbyists' reef aquariums as long as they are not eaten by tank mates.

Chromis

Blue Reef Chromis (*Chromis cyaneus*), Blue Green Chromis (*Chromis viridis*), Sunshine Chromis (*Chromis insolata*) and Yellow Chromis (*Chromis analis*)

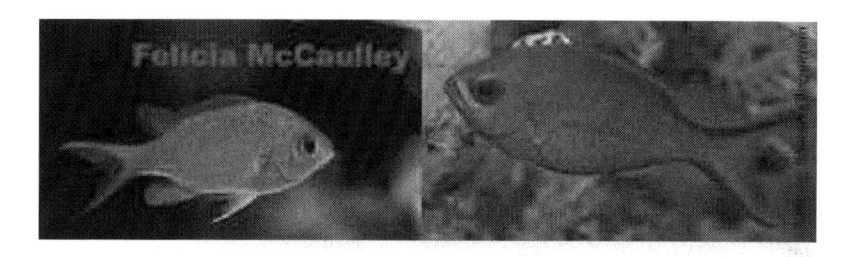

Blue Green and Blue Reef Chromis

Chromis are peaceful fish, ideal for those who prefer schooling fish. Chromis look similar to damsel fish but they definitely do not have the aggressive bullying behavior.

Most Chromis stay out in the open usually swimming in the upper portion of an aquarium. They prefer to be in schools which apparently appeal to their sense of security. If something scares them they will disperse and dash inside the rock work or decorations.

Most Chromis grow to three inches long, but Blue Reef Chromis grow to about five inches long. The peaceful nature of Chromis makes them easy to mix with nonaggressive fish, although you may see them quarreling among themselves. Chromis are safe with corals and invertebrates.

Chromis are carnivorous and will readily eat any food that is put in the aquarium.

Clownfish

Clarkii Clownfish (*Amphiprion clarkii*), Maroon Clownfish (*Premnas biaculeatus*), Ocellaris Clownfish (*Amphiprion ocellaris*), Orange Skunk Clownfish (*Amphiprion sandaracinos*), Pink Skunk Clownfish (*Amphiprion perideraion*), Tomato Clownfish (*Amphiprion frenatus*) and True Percula Clownfish (*Amphiprion percula*)

Ocellaris and Pink Skunk Clownfish

Snowflake and Black Ocellaris Clownfish

Clownfish - especially since the movie *Finding Nemo* - are the most recognized and commonly kept of all saltwater fish. The movie stars the top-selling Ocellaris Clownfish with a strikingly deep-orange body and bright white stripes. Clownfish can be pink, yellow, black, maroon or red, and most have white stripes. They are hardy and easy to keep, making them great starter fish for a beginning hobbyist. Many Clownfish are hatched and raised in captivity. These fish are generally hardier than wild caught and more easily assimilate into new aquariums than their wild-caught counterparts.

Clownfish are generally excellent additions to any saltwater aquarium including living reefs although some Clownfish species become very aggressive towards their tank mates as they mature. Another possible downside to housing Clownfish in a reef aquarium is that occasionally one of these magnificent creatures will settle on using the polyps of a coral to burrow into when no sea anemone is present. A Clownfish residing in live coral may cause its coral to keep its polyps partially or completely retracted. Therefore the coral may starve.

Clownfish with Anemone

Many people have seen pictures of Clownfish hiding or playing in the tentacles of a sea anemone. While Clownfish use anemones for protection in the wild, they can live well in a saltwater aquarium with or without an anemone.

Sea anemones have drawbacks of which hobbyist should be aware. When you place a sea anemone in the very spot that it looks great, you have little guarantee that it will stay put! Anemones are more mobile than one would think, and will move wherever they want, often ending up in a place that is hard to see. They may even stick to the glass of the aquarium! Another challenge to housing an anemone is that they can sting and kill corals. For this reason alone, most reef hobbyists choose to keep just a Clownfish or two without an anemone.

Clownfish are protandrous hermaphrodites, meaning that these fish are born male and turn into females. When adding two Clownfish to an aquarium, choose two different-sized fish. The larger, more dominant fish will slowly develop into a female if it is not already. The female will be more aggressive than the male, attacking or chasing off other fish that wander into their territory.

Most Clownfish do best when kept alone or in pairs. A pair can aggressively protect their territory. Only add one species of Clownfish to your aquarium. If you add different species in the same aquarium the most aggressive Clownfish can kill off less dominant Clownfish.

Most Clownfish will grow to about three inches while some species can grow up to seven inches in length. Clownfish are generally hardy eaters and the first ones to the dinner table. Clownfish are omnivorous and will eat almost any saltwater food that hits the water.

Damselfish

Azure Damselfish (*Chrysiptera hemicyanea*), Blue Damselfish (*Chrysiptera cyanea*), Talbot's Damselfish (*Chrysiptera talboti*), Three Spot Domino Damselfish (Dascyllus trimaculatus), Three Stripe Damselfish (Dascyllus aruanus), Yellowtail Damselfish (*Chrysiptera parasema*) and Yellow Damselfish (*Amblyglyphidodon aureus*)

Azure and Yellow Tailed Damsel

Damselfish are very popular among beginning hobbyists because of their bright colors and inexpensive price. Unfortunately, damsel fish are territorial and constantly chase each other. This constant bullying behavior can take away the enjoyment and calming effect of watching your aquarium.

If you prefer a passive aquarium it is best to skip Damselfish and choose calm, peaceful, schooling Chromis. That said, Damselfish are extremely hardy and easy to keep. Most become very territorial as they mature and often exhibit aggressive behavior towards tank mates and new fish. It is vital to have an abundance of caves and crevices for these fish to claim. Remember that adding fish to an aquarium with live rock is the easy part; trying to catch a fish can be VERY difficult and the entire rock work may have to be dismantled. Choose carefully before introducing any fish!

Yellowtail Damselfish are among the least aggressive. They are beautiful, with their bright blue bodies and bright yellow tails. They are usually peaceful towards tank mates, although may quarrel among themselves.

Damselfish are active swimmers and most of the Damsels listed above will grow up to three inches long.

Damsels are omnivores, are not picky and will eagerly eat either frozen or dry foods. They are safe to keep with corals and invertebrates.

Dartfish

Blue Gudgeon (*Ptereleotris heteroptera*), Firefish (Nemateleotris magnifica), Purple Firefish (Nemateleotris decora), Scissortail (Ptereleotris evides) and Zebra Barred (Ptereleotris zebra)

NOTE: For this discussion, Dartfish are separated by Genus into two sections.

Dartfish (Genus Ptereleotris)

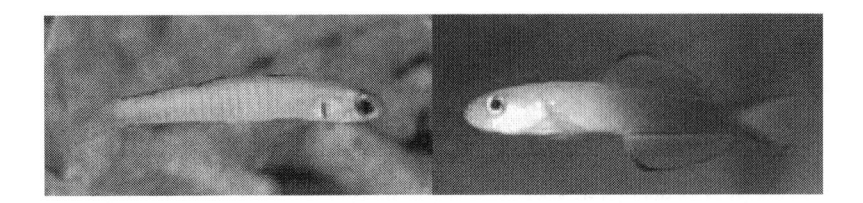

Zebra Barred and Scissortail

Dartfish are a great group of fish for peaceful aquariums. These elongated fish are hardy, nonaggressive and easy to care for and safe to mix with corals and invertebrates.

Dartfish can be kept singularly or in pairs, however they do best as a group of a single species. The group usually hangs around the middle of the aquarium and needs lots of caves and crevices to make a hasty retreat when frightened. Species like the Blue Gudgeon will make a burrow in the sand and dart into their burrow for protection.

Depending on the species, some can grow to a maximum of four inches while others can grow up to five and half inches long. Keep these peaceful fish with other nonaggressive fish.

Their elongated body allows them to be great jumpers, so be sure your aquarium has an enclosed lid or you'll find them dried up on your floor!

Dartfish are carnivores and will eat both frozen and dry meaty foods. They stay out in the open always on the lookout for food. Even though they are meat eaters, they are safe to mix with invertebrates and corals.

Firefish (Genus Nemateleotris spp.)

Firefish and Purple Firefish

Firefish are hardy, peaceful and easy to keep. These delicate looking fish are elongated, very colorful and have a distinctive long back fin (dorsal ray).

These fish need caves and crevices to feel secure. When threatened they will shoot into the live rock or an ornament. Also when frightened they can jump out of the aquarium and plunge to their death. An enclosed top is a must for this quick moving escape artist!

Firefish grow to a length of two and half or three inches long depending on the species. It is best to keep one fish or a male and female. If adding more than two Firefish, one will quickly become dominant over the others and begin bullying and nipping fins. This can ultimately lead to death for the less aggressive fish.

Dottyback

Bicolor Dottyback (*Pictichromis paccagnellae*), Indigo Dottyback (*Pseudochromis fridmani x sankeyi*), Neon Dottyback (*Pseudochromis aldabraensis*), Orchid Dottyback (*Pseudochromis fridmani*), Purple Stripe Dottyback (*Pseudochromis diadema*), Springeri Dottyback (*Pseudochromis springerii*) and Sunrise Dottyback (*Pseudochromis flavivertex*)

Orchid and Purple Stripe Dottyback

Several Dottyback species have bright striking purple and/or intense yellow colors. Most stay small and tank-raised Dottybacks are very hardy.

Dottybacks need lots of caves and crevices so that they can choose their hiding place as many enjoy swimming in and out of rocks. Dottybacks will defend their hiding place from intruders. Though smaller Dottybacks only grow to about three inches long they are able defend their territories against much larger fish. The Indigo Dottyback is an exception; it has a peaceful demeanor. The other extreme is the Royal Dottyback which can be very aggressive towards other tank mates.

In general, keep only one Dottyback in an aquarium as they are aggressive towards their own species. It is possible to keep several Dottybacks in large aquariums with lots of rock work.

Some Dottybacks are free swimmers while other will not venture far from their rock crevice or cave. When startled, they will dart back to their hiding place. Many species are tank-raised and will adjust quickly to your aquarium.

Dottybacks are carnivores; tank-raised varieties will readily eat frozen or dry foods. They also eat any worms and other tiny critters they may find in the aquarium. Several species are beneficial because they will consume dreaded bristle worms which come in on live rock. Dottybacks are safe with corals but may eat small invertebrates; they can harass and are known to kill shrimp.

Eels

Green Wolf Eel (Congrogadus subducens), Snowflake Eel (Echidna nebulosa), Tessalata Eel (Gymnothorax favagineus), Zebra Moray Eel (Gymnomuraena zebra)

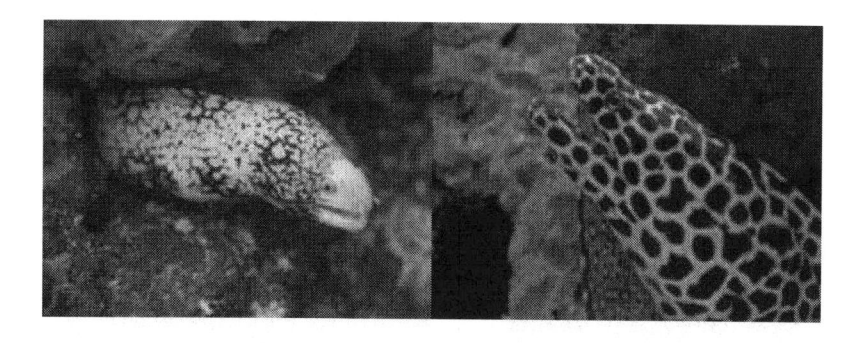

Snowflake Moray and Tessalata Eel (Gymnothorax favagineus)

The eel species listed above include some of the most popular and best Eels to keep in home aquariums. These eels are attractive, hardy and easy to keep. Eels should be kept in aquariums with plenty of hiding places to help them feel secure. Many of these master escape artists have climbed out of their aquariums to untimely deaths, so to keep your Eel safe, make certain the top of your aquarium is fully covered.

Since the species of eels listed above have different requirements they will be discussed separately.

Green Wolf Eel

Green Wolf Eels or Carpet Eel Blennies are fish that look like, are named like, and are commonly mistaken for eels. A Green Wolf Eels is actually a pseudochromid (Dottyback).

Green Wolf Eels grow to a maximum length of almost 18 inches, and require an aquarium of at least 55 gallons. They need a meaty diet consisting of foods like krill, shrimp, squid and other frozen and live fish. They generally are quick to learn to eat in captivity, but if you happen to have a finicky eater, feed it live glass shrimp, small feeder guppies, tuffies or goldfish, depending on the size of the food and eel.

To keep aggression down and the aquarium clean, try to feed frozen or prepared foods instead of live.

Their colors range from a bright green to a mottled light brown. This eel will do well in aquariums with tangs, angels, dwarf lion fish, large clown fish and much more. As a rule, keep the Wolf Eel with semi-aggressive to aggressive fish, one Green Wolf Eel to an aquarium.

Snowflake Moray Eel

The Snowflake Eel is the most commonly kept eel in home aquariums. This beautifully patterned fish is reasonably priced, adapts quickly to aquarium life and remains relatively small. Snowflake eels are generally for sale in tiny sizes and can grow to over two feet long in the home aquarium. These eels require a large aquarium with dimensions of at least three feet by two feet.

These meat eaters will enjoy a variety of foods including krill, shrimp, squid and frozen fish. They will also eat live crustaceans like shrimp and small fish if they can catch them. Best kept with medium to larger fish, Snowflake eels are compatible with a few invertebrates, including feather dusters, sea anemones and corals.

Zebra Moray Eel

Zebra Moray Eels have a beautiful banded pattern giving them a striking appearance. Their bodies are much thicker than snowflake eels. This eel requires a very large aquarium as it can grow up to five feet in length. Although large, it has a laid back personality and will not normally eat its tank mates with the exception of crustaceans, such as ornamental shrimp, which they may consider a delicacy.

Depending on the size of the eel it can require large chunks of meaty marine foods like krill, shrimp, squid, clams and frozen and fresh fish. Make sure this eel is eating before purchasing.

NOTE: This eel will also be less active in the aquarium than a snowflake moray.

Tessalata Eel

The Tessalata eel is included in our list because it is awesome. That said it will only be kept by a few hobbyists not only because of its large size and predatory behavior limits its fish mates, but also because it requires a very large aquarium. Their beautiful pattern makes them popular among large eel hobbyists.

This eel can grow to well over five feet in length and should be kept in an aquarium with dimensions of at least six long by two feet wide. As mentioned, they are predatory and will eat small to medium size fish and most crustaceans. A Tessalata makes a good tank mate for large, aggressive fish. Caution should be taken when cleaning the aquarium to ensure you do not get a nasty bite.

Like other eels, these eels require a diet of seafood including fresh and frozen fish, squid, shrimp and other meaty foods.

Gobies

Bluespotted Watchman Goby (*Cryptocentrus pavoninoides*), Clown Goby (*Gobiodon citrinus*), Clown Goby, Green (*Gobiodon atrangulatus*), Clown Goby, Yellow (*Gobiodon okinawae*), Court Jester Goby (*Amblygobius rainfordi*), Diagonal Bar Prawn Goby (*Amblyeleotris diagonalis*), Diamond Watchman Goby (*Valenciennea puellaris*), Engineer Goby (*Pholidichthys leucotaenia*), Hector's Goby (*Amblygobius hectori*), Hi Fin Red Banded Goby (*Stonogobiops nematodes*), Neon Goby (*Elacatinus oceanops*), Orange Spotted Goby (*Amblyeleotris guttata*), Orange Stripe Prawn Goby (*Amblyeleotris randalli*), Pink Spotted Watchman Goby(*Cryptocentrus leptocephalus*), Pinkbar Goby (*Amblyeleotris aurora*), Red Head Goby (*Elacatinus puncticulatus*), Sleeper Banded Goby (*Amblygobius phalaena*), Sleeper Gold Head Goby (*Valenciennea strigata*), Tiger Watchman Goby (*Valenciennea wardii*), Two Spot Goby (*Signigobius biocellatus*), Wheeler's Shrimp Goby (*Amblyeleotris wheeleri*), Yasha White Ray Shrimp Goby (*Stonogobiops yasha*) and Yellow Watchman Goby (*Cryptocentrus cinctus*)

Yellow Clown and Orange Stripe Prawn Goby

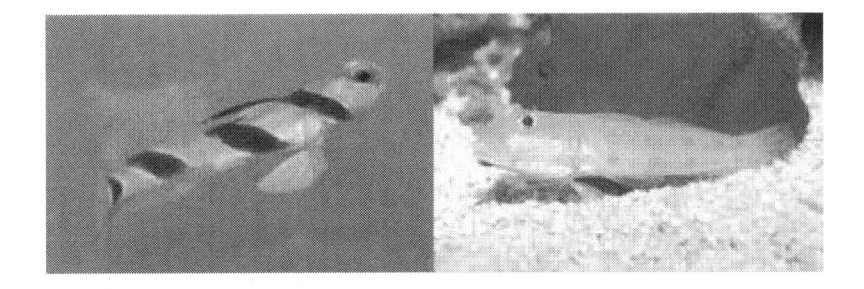

High Fin Red Banded and Diamond Goby

Gobies are a huge family comprising over 2000 different species of fish. Therefore the information discussed here will be very general and based on the species listed above. Many gobies will grow to one and a half to around six inches long. Most are easy to keep and peaceful. Nearly all Gobies (except Sleeper Gobies) have a pelvic sucking disc, which in the ocean allows them to attach to rocks and not get swept away by the current. In the home aquarium, they will either perch on rocks with their disc and may even attach themselves to the aquarium glass.

Most Gobies stay in the lower portion of the aquarium and some dig burrows in the sand. Rockwork will provide numerous spots for Gobies to hide and feel comfortable. Most Gobies are relatively small with an elongated body enabling them to be good jumpers. Make sure you have an enclosed top on your aquarium.

One of the most fascinating characteristics about some Gobies is their symbiotic relationship with pistol shrimp. A shrimp and Goby will live together in a burrow which the shrimp excavated. The shrimp will maintain the burrow while the Goby stands guard near the entrance. When a predator comes near, the Goby alerts the shrimp. They both will hide in the burrow until the danger is gone. They will also sleep together in their burrow.

Yasha White Ray Shrimp Goby and Candy Stripe Pistol Shrimp

A few Gobies that mix with pistol shrimps are Hi Fin Red Banded Gobies, Yasha White Ray Shrimp Gobies and Yellow Watchman Gobies. A few pistol shrimps which make great companions are Tiger Snapping, Snapping, and Red Banded Shrimp.

Grouper
Blue Line Grouper (Cephalopholis formosa), Bluespotted Grouper (Cephalopholis argus), Miniatus Grouper (Cephalopholis miniatus), Panther Grouper (Cromileptes altivelis), V-tail Grouper (Cephalopholis urodeta)

Blue Spotted and Miniatus Grouper

Most Groupers make great pets for large aquariums and are among the hardiest of all saltwater fish. One of the most striking Groupers is the Miniatus with its bright red head and body dotted with bright blue spots.

Most Grouper species listed above require a large aquarium of at least two feet wide by six feet long. As a group these fish are semi-aggressive to aggressive and most species should only be kept one per aquarium. Make sure you have plenty of hiding places for a Grouper to feel secure. Most will be aggressive towards tank mates that enter their hiding place.

There are many fish that will do well with groupers including larger Angelfish, Lionfish, Tangs, Triggerfish, Wrasse and Eels. Whichever tank mates you choose, make sure they are too large to fit in your grouper's mouth or they could become an expensive meal.

Panther Groupers are extremely popular. Juveniles are adorable with their unique pearl white bodies, dark spots and flowing fins. Panthers are passive towards tank mates; however this fish grows quickly and many times can outgrow an aquarium. Panther Groupers will reach lengths of well over twelve inches and, like most Groupers, can swallow any fish that will fit in their extremely large mouth. Groupers are carnivores, safe with corals but will eat ornamental shrimps, crabs and other invertebrates. Feed them a varied diet of fresh and frozen fish, shrimp, clams, mollusk, scallops, squid and other seafood.

Hawkfish

Arc Eye Hawkfish (Paracirrhitus arcuatus), Falco Hawkfish (Cirrhitichthys falco), Flame Hawkfish (Neocirrhitus armatus), Freckled Hawkfish (Paracirrhites forsteri), Longnose Hawkfish (Oxycirrhites typus), Pixy Hawkfish (Cirrhitichthys oxycephalus)

Longnose and Falco Hawkfish

Hawkfish are hardy, easy to care for and most have attractive patterns and interesting personalities. Their descriptive name comes from the fact that many species of this interesting fish can be found perching on high rock formations in the aquarium and will swoop down to grab food like a hawk.

Hawkfish are not for every aquarium. By nature they are territorial and can harass their tank mates, eat smaller fish, shrimp and some crabs. The Flame Hawk is one of the most popular species because of its striking red color; full grown it will be less than four inches long. The Falco, Flame and Longnose are among the least aggressive of the Hawk Fish.

Freckled Hawkfish can grow quite large (up to nine inches long) and are aggressive. It is territorial and can harass its tank mates. On the other hand, Falco Hawkfish stay small - a little over two inches long - and are one of the least aggressive species.

As a general rule, keep only one Hawkfish in your aquarium. Make sure you provide them plenty of caves or crevices in which to hide and feel secure. These healthy eaters prefer a variety of meaty foods including shrimp, krill and squid, live or chopped up fish and even some dry foods.

Jawfish

Black Cap (*Opistognathus randalli*), Blue Dot (*Opistognathus rosenblatti*), Dusky (*Opistognathus whitehursti*), Pearly (*Opistognathus aurifrons*) , Tiger (*Opistognathus sp.*) and Yellowhead (*Opistognathus aurifrons*)

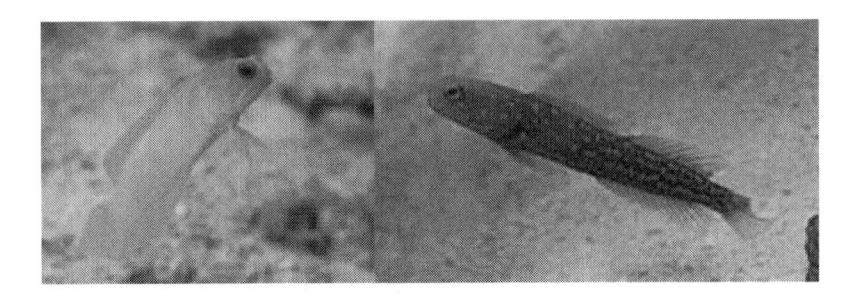

Pearly and Blue Dot Jawfish

Jawfish are peaceful and fun to watch as they build and take care of their home. Jawfish are easy to recognize with their elongated body, long continuous fin on top and under their bodies, a huge mouth, and very large eyes. Their huge mouth is used to dig their home.

Jawfish create their homes by digging a burrow in the sand. They literally take mouthfuls of sand and spit it out somewhere else in the aquarium. Reef aquarium hobbyist beware with corals close by the burrow can be covered in expelled sand. They will continue moving the sand until a tunnel is created. The Jawfish will spend much time in his burrow with just his head peeking out. If a fish swims near the burrow, the Jawfish will try to chase it away.

To construct the burrow the Jawfish needs various size sand, rubble and small shells or pieces of shells. Since Jawfish can dig under the rockwork it is best to stack the rock in the aquarium before adding the sand so that the Jawfish cannot burrow under the rockwork and cause the rocks to tumble.

Jawfish, depending on species, will grow to three and a half to four inches in length. Again, depending on the species, you can keep more than one in an aquarium. When startled, Jawfish will either dart back to their burrow or they may jump out of the aquarium. Keep the top of your aquarium covered.

Jawfish are carnivores. During feeding time, they will dart in and out of their burrow. Some species will eat invertebrates but all are safe with corals.

Mandarin

Green Mandarin (*Synchiropus splendidus*), Spotted Mandarin (*Synchiropus picturatus*) and Red Mandarin (*Synchiropus cf. splendidus*)

Green Mandarin

Green and Red Mandarins are some of the most beautiful, colorful fish with unique patterns you will find in the ocean. Mandarins make fish for reef aquariums since they are safe to keep with corals and invertebrates.

These fish are fun to watch as they scoot around the sand and live rock looking for food. Wild-caught Mandarins are difficult to keep alive long-term in an saltwater aquarium because they forage for amphipods and copepods which is usually not present in a home aquarium and may not be as abundant in a home reef aquarium as they are in the ocean. In established reefs, and with a refugium, it is possible for wild-caught Mandarins to find enough food; it is also possible to supplement these foods with commercial packaged amphipods and copepods. This can be a lot of work for a hobbyist (continually adding live foods) and, sadly, most wild-caught Mandarins starve to death over time. Choosing tank-raised Mandarins can eliminate this difficulty and most will devour a variety of frozen and dry foods.

Mandarins are fun to watch and will live with a variety of nonaggressive saltwater fish. They stay small, grow to three and a half to four inches long, and can be found in three colors, each with unique patterns. Males are easy to recognize by their long first dorsal spine. Do not keep two males together - they will fight!

CAUTION: Mandarins have a sharp spine on their cheeks which can get caught in a fish net. To transport, herd these little fish into a plastic container.

Tang

Blonde Naso Tang (*Naso elegans*), Blue Tang (*Paracanthurus hepatus*), Bristletooth Tomini Tang (*Ctenochaetus tominiensis*), Chevron Tang (*Ctenochaetus hawaiiensis*), Convict Tang (*Acanthurus triostegus*), Desjardini (*Zebrasoma desjardini*), Kole Yellow Eye Tang (*Ctenochaetus strigosus*), Lieutenant Tang (*Acanthurus tennenti*), Orangeshoulder Tang (*Acanthurus olivaceous*), Naso Tang (*Naso lituratus*), Powder Blue Tang (*Acanthurus leucosternon*), Purple Tang (*Zebrasoma xanthurum*), Sailfin Tang (*Zebrasoma veliferum*), Scopas Tang (*Zebrasoma scopas*), Vlamingii Tang (*Naso vlamingii*), Whitecheek Tang (*Acanthurus nigricans*) and Hawaiian Yellow Tang (*Zebrasoma flavescens*)

Powder Blue and Yellow Tang

Sailfin and Pacific Blue Tang

Tangs are so popular that almost every saltwater aquarium has at least one and often times it is the largest fish in the aquarium. Tangs are often called surgeonfish, a name derived from the scalpel-like spines on both sides of their bodies just before their tail. These spines are an instrument of defense to protect themselves and their territories.

Tangs can aggressively defend their territory against fish with similar body shapes and colors. Generally keep one Tang per tank. Larger aquariums can keep multiple Tangs as long as they have different shapes, colors and sizes. For instance, an elongated Pacific Blue Tang will usually live well in an aquarium with the more rounded Yellow Tang. It is also possible to keep schools of the same species of Tangs in large aquariums if they are introduced into the aquarium at the same time.

One of the most popular Tangs is the Blue Tang. Like *Nemo* the clownfish, this fish became famous as *Dory* in the movie *Finding Nemo*. This movie created such an interest in the Blue Tang that it became one of the most sought after fish in aquarium stores. Even today, long after the movie's popularity peaked, Blue Tangs remain one of the bestselling species of fish available.

Most adult Tangs require an aquarium of at least 75 gallons. Blue Tangs are both beautiful and hardy, but can grow quite large. It is not unusual to find Blue Tangs up to a foot long in the ocean; Vlamingii Tangs often grow to two feet long in the wild! The smallest Tang in our list above is the Bristletooth Tomini Tang, which grows to six inches long. Since Tangs are found in such a huge range of sizes, research your favorite species before making a purchase to make sure the tang you choose will not outgrow your aquarium.

Tangs are active swimmers so always ensure the rock is stacked to provide plenty of holes and spaces for them to swim. Many Tangs spend their days grazing the live rock looking for algae. Tangs are herbivores and generally good eaters. Feed them a diet rich in algae and other vegetables. Supplement their diet by feeding Nori algae sheets once or twice a week.

There are a few Tangs, such as Chevron, Convict, Bristletooth Tomini, Whitecheek and Hawaiian Yellow, which are safe with both corals and invertebrates.

Triggerfish

Blue Throat Triggerfish (Xanthichthys auromarginatus), Bluelined Triggerfish (Pseudobalistes fuscus), Bursa Triggerfish (Rhinecanthus verrucosus), Clown Triggerfish (Balistoides conspicillum), Crosshatch Triggerfish (Xanthichthys mento), Humu Humu Triggerfish (Rhinecanthus aculeatus), Niger Triggerfish (Odonus niger), Pinktail Triggerfish (Melichthys vidua), Rectangle Triggerfish (Rhinecanthus rectangulus), Sargassum (Xanthichthys sp.), Undulate Triggerfish (Balistapus undulatus)

Niger and Humu Humu Triggerfish

Undulate and Clown Triggerfish

Triggerfish are hardy, easy to care for, and adapt readily to the home aquarium. They are, however, rather aggressive. Their name comes from their second dorsal fin called a trigger spine which locks erect their first dorsal fin. These fins allow Triggerfish to wedge themselves into rock crevices, coral or anything stationary when they are threatened or just want to rest.

Most Triggerfish are very territorial and some, as they mature, become downright mean. A few of the least aggressive species are Humu Humu and Odonus Niger Triggerfish. Two of the most aggressive are the Clown and Undulated Triggerfish. As a rule, even less aggressive triggers should be kept with semi-aggressive and aggressive tank mates. Each triggerfish has its own personality and sometimes some of the most aggressive species may be less antagonistic than normal. It is often wise to add the most aggressive fish to an aquarium last, allowing less hostile fish time to acclimate and choose their territories.

Since most Triggers grow to at least six to eight inches long they require an aquarium of at least 90 gallons. Add plenty of decorations or rockwork for fish to hide and feel secure. Fewer places to hide can lead to more aggressive fish. Tank mates for the Triggerfish can include large Angelfish, large Hawkfish, Groupers, Tangs, Lionfish and Eels.

Most Triggerfish are carnivores and will readily eat small fish, shrimp, sea urchins, worms, crabs and other invertebrates. Feed them a varied diet at least twice a day of fresh and frozen fish, shrimp, clams, mollusk, scallops, squid and other seafood. Some Triggerfish are omnivorous and should have marine algae and other prepared herbivore foods added to their diet.

Blue Throat, Sargassum and Crosshatch Triggerfish may be kept in a reef aquarium since they will not bother the corals but, as mentioned they can eat small fish and invertebrates.

CAUTION: On the body, directly before the tail, Triggerfish have spike-like rows of spines. These small spines can get caught in a fish net. Use a fine mesh fish net and be careful when removing them from the net so as not to damage their scales.

Wrasse

For our purposes, Wrasses will be separated into two main groups:
- Wrasses for fish only aquariums
- Wrasses for reef safe/community aquariums

Wrasses are generally safe to keep with corals, however many can eat small fish and a variety of invertebrates which makes them a poor choice for reef aquariums.

Wrasse for Fish Only Aquariums

Banana Wrasse (Thalassoma lutescens), Bird Wrasse (Gomphosus varius), Bluehead Wrasse (Thalassoma bifasciatum),

Lyretail Wrasse (Thalassoma lunare), Paddlefin Wrasse (Thalassoma lucasanum), Yellow Wrasse (Halichoeres chrysus)

Lunare and Green Bird Wrasse (Male)

Most of the above listed Wrasse species are semi-aggressive to very aggressive in nature, hardy and easy to care for. These fish make great additions to aquariums with fishes such as Angels, Puffers, Tangs and less aggressive Triggerfish.

Most of these Wrasses are beautifully colorful. They are active swimmers and need plenty of open space to swim as well as rock work or caves in which to hide. They are normally territorial and may aggravate new fish, therefore, depending on its tank mates, it may be best to save this fish so that it is one of the last fish added to your aquarium. Their streamlined bodies make them efficient jumpers. Be sure the top of your aquarium is completely and securely covered.

Many of the above Wrasses will be aggressive towards smaller fish. These carnivores will eat small fish, small shrimp, snails, tube worms and some will even eat crabs. Hence, keep them full and happy with a meaty diet of fresh and frozen shrimp, fish, krill, clams, scallops and other seafood.

Wrasse for Reef Safe /Community Aquariums

Carpenter's Flasher Wrasse (*Paracheilinus carpenteri*), Eightline Wrasse (*Pseudocheilinus octotaenia*), Exquisite Fairy Wrasse (*Cirrhilabrus exquisitus*), Labout's Fairy Wrasse (*Cirrhilabrus laboutei*), Lineatus Fairy Wrasse (*Cirrhilabrus lineatus*), Longfin Fairy Wrasse (*Cirrhilabrus rubriventralis*), Lubbock's Fairy Wrasse (*Cirrhilabrus lubbocki*), McCosker's Flasher Wrasse (*Paracheilinus mccoskeri*), Mystery Wrasse (*Pseudocheilinus ocellatus*), Pink Margin Fairy Wrasse (*Cirrhilabrus rubrimarginatus*), Red Velvet Fairy Wrasse (Cirrhilabrus *rubrisquamis*), Scott's Fairy Wrasse (*Cirrhilabrus scottorum*), Six Line Wrasse (Pseudocheilinus *hexataenia*), Solorensis Fairy Wrasse (*Cirrhilabrus solorensis*), Yellow Banded Possum Wrasse (*Wetmorella nigropinnata*), Whip Fin Fairy Wrasse (*Cirrhilabrus filamentosus*) and White Banded Possum Wrasse (*Wetmorella albofasciata*)

The Wrasse family is huge and offers some amazing gems for a reef aquarium. Reef safe wrasses are very diverse, therefore they are divided up into a number of different Genus. Since Wrasses from the same Genus have similar requirements we will discuss them by Genus. We will only discuss the best and safest Genus for a reef aquarium.

Longfin Fairy Wrasse

Wrasses of the Genus Cirrhilabrus are called Fairy Wrasses. These are typically very active, peaceful fish; male Fairy Wrasses have truly amazing colors. Males are much more colorful than the females. Once acclimated to a reef, they will readily eat meaty foods. A Fairy Wrasse will make a mucus cocoon to protect it while sleeping among the rockwork. A couple of great choices are Solorensis Fairy Wrasse and Labout's Fairy Wrasse; both are hardy, colorful and safe with corals and invertebrates.

McCosker's Flasher Wrasse

Wrasses of the Genus Paracheilinus are called Flasher Wrasses. The name comes from the way a male Wrasse "flashes" when courting or protecting its territory. While flashing, he spreads out his top fin and tail fin as blood rushes to the scales creating a beautiful colorful display. The Flashers have similar characteristics to the Fairy Wrasses except they are smaller. Flashers also have hearty appetites and eat meaty foods. Males are more colorful than the females. The Flasher Wrasse will also create a mucus cocoon when it sleeps among the rockwork.

Six Line Wrasse

Wrasses of the Genus Pseudocheilinus are called Lined Wrasses. Popular members of this group are the four and six line Wrasses. These fish are very hardy and stay small. Lined Wrasses spend their time searching out and eating flatworms and other pests in reef aquariums. The downside is that, when mature, they usually become pugnacious and bully new tank mates as well as other Wrasses. The Lined Wrasse will also create a mucus cocoon when it sleeps among the rockwork.

Yellow Banded Possum Wrasse

Wrasses of the Genus Wetmorella are called Possum Wrasses. These Wrasses are great for small reef aquariums, growing only to two and a half inches long. They are very hardy and easy to care for. A Yellow-Banded Possum Wrasse is a peaceful, secretive little fish which hides in the rock work. They are safe with corals and invertebrates.

There are a few general requirements for all of these reef safe Wrasses. Tank mates of reef safe Wrasses should be relatively peaceful fish. Wrasses are good jumpers and need an enclosed top on the aquarium. Since Wrasses are very active, they should be fed a meaty diet several times a day. All the above Wrasses are safe with corals. Invertebrates may become food for many of the Wrasses with exception of the Possum Wrasses.

There are a lot of reef safe Wrasses and most have different requirements. Before buying a Wrasse by its exotic beauty alone, make sure it will thrive in your aquarium.

A Few Rules for Stocking Your Aquarium

As you can see, there are many fish that do well in saltwater aquariums. The biggest challenge that new and even experienced hobbyists have is figuring out which fish can be mixed together. Since each fish has their own personality, they sometimes break general rules. On the following pages are examples of groups of fish that should live long lives together.

A general rule of thumb when you begin stocking your new aquarium is to put about 1/2 inch of fish per four gallons of aquarium water. It is best to introduce new fish to your aquarium after it has been running for 24 hours. These will be the only fish you add until after the aquarium has Cycled and you have completed your first water change.

A general guide line for a fully stocked non aggressive aquarium is about 1/2 inch of fish per gallon of aquarium water. It is always better to under stock an aquarium than to overstock. On the following pages, you will find the maximum size of the fish grown in an aquarium beside the name of the fish. In the wild, most of these fish can get much larger.

Examples of Fully Stocked Aquariums

29 gallon Aquarium
Use 5-7 fish, 2-3 Inches long

1 Cherub Angel (3")
1 Pajama Cardinal (3")
1 Chalk Bass (3")
1 Yellow Watchman Goby (3")
1 Yellow Tail Blue Damsels (2.5")
OR
2 Ocellaris Clownfish (3.5")
1 Royal Gramma (3")
1 Banggai Cardinalfish (3")
1 Bicolor Blenny (4")

38 gallon Aquarium
Use 5-8 fish, 2-4 Inches long

1 Coral Beauty Angelfish (4")
2 Ocellaris Clownfish (3.5")
1 Royal Gramma (3")
1 Six Line Wrasse (3")
1 Yellow Tail Blue Damsel (2.5")
OR
1 Rusty Angelfish (3.5")
1 Pink Skunk Clownfish (3")
3 Threadfin Cardinalfish (2")
1 Canary Wrasse (4")
1 Fire Fish goby (3.5")
OR
1 Valentini Puffer (4")
2 Ocellaris Clownfish (3.5")
1 Six Line Wrasse (3")
1 Signal Goby (3")

1 Green Chromis (3")
OR
1 Yellow Candy Hogfish (4")
1 Chalk Bass (3")
1 Flame Cardinalfish (3.5")
1 Barnacle Blenny (2")
1 Yellow Tail Blue Damsel (2.5")
1 Falco Hawkfish (2.5")

55 gallon Aquarium
Use 5-9 fish, 3-6 Inches long

1 Flame Angel (3.9")
1 Kole Tang (5.5")
1 Clarkii Clownfish (5")
3 Green Chromis (3")
1 Diamond Watchman Goby (6")
OR
1 Lamark Angel (5.5")
1 Tomini Tang (7")
1 Tomato Clownfish (4.5")
1 Flame Hawk fish (3.5")
1 Paddlefin Wrasse (6")
1 Valentini Puffer (4")

90 gallon Aquarium
Use 5-9 fish, 5-6 Inches long

1 Koran Angelfish (7")
2 Clarkii Clownfish (5")
1 Tomini Tang (7")
3 Pajama Cardinal (3")
1 Arc Eye Hawk (4.5")
1 Solorensis Wrasse (5")

3 Green Chromis (3")

OR

1 Bellus Angelfish (6")
1 Tomato Clownfish (5")
1 Yellow Tang (7")
1 Starry Blenny (5")
1 Green Bird Wrasse (8")
1 Odonus Niger Trigger (7")
1 Foxface Lo* (8")

OR

Aggressive
1 Passer Angelfish (8")
1 Humu Humu Trigger (8")
1 Freckled Hawkfish (8")
1 Lyretail Wrasse (7")
1 Desjardinii Tang (8")

125-150 gallon Aquarium

Use 7-9 fish, 6-8 Inches long

1 Majestic Angel (8")
1 Maroon Clownfish (6")
1 Striped Squirrelfish (7")
1 Dog Face Puffer (8")
1 Freckled Hawkfish (9")
1 Green Bird Wrasse (8")
1 Desjardini Tang (9")
1 Snowflake Eel (24")

OR

1 Passer Angelfish (8")
1 Banana Wrasse (8")
1 Sailfin Tang (8")
1 Blue Hippo Tang (9")
2 Clarkii Clownfish (5")
1 Spotted Hawkfish (5")

* Foxface Lo fish have venomous spines. Be careful when transporting fish and when cleaning your aquarium to avoid the possibility of being stung.

TIP: When choosing fish find out how large they will grow. You will want them to fit into your aquarium!

DOWNLOAD YOUR FREE BONUSES: "Livestock Tracking Sheet" and "My Perfect Fish Identifier" at http://9nl.be/Freebonuses

Bringing Your New Fish Home

Now that you have purchased your fish, you want to keep them happy and healthy. Your fish will be sealed in a water and air-filled plastic bag with rubber bands or clasps holding the top closed. The parameters in the fish transportation bag (pH, salinity, temperature, etc.) may be different from your aquarium. New fish will do best if they are slowly acclimated to their new environment.

There are three methods to introduce your new fish into your saltwater aquarium and the method you choose is based on how long and how many fish were carried in their transportation bag. The longer the fish is left in the bag, the more stress it will endure. Stress can be caused by temperature change, rough handling, low oxygen levels and toxin build up in the water. Fish excrete toxic ammonia through their gills as well as in their waste and urine. Inside a closed fish bag an interesting thing can occur: over time, pH drops converting toxic ammonia to a less toxic ammonium. When the fish bag is opened, CO_2 (which is acid) escapes, the pH rises, and ammonium converts back into toxic ammonia.

One popular acclimation method used by many hobbyists is to place the water from the fish bag, along with the new fish, in a bucket. Using airline tubing, they will allow water from their aquarium to slowly drip into this bucket. The challenge with this method is that if the fish has been in the shipping bag for more than a couple of hours, a sizeable amount of ammonia and ammonium will have accumulated. Since the pH of a saltwater aquarium is typically above 8.0, while this water slowly drips into the bucket, the low pH in the bucket water rises. Research has found that ammonium is not readily taken into a fish's body, but ammonia easily passes through the fishes gills into the bloodstream. Then the fish's body converts this ammonia to ammonium. Inside the body ammonium causes damage affecting the central nervous system which manifests symptoms of fish darting and sinking.

If you still prefer to drip acclimate your fish which have been in their shipping water for long periods of time, use an ammonia binding agent which are readily available from several aquarium manufacturers. Ammonia binding agents are used for treating municipal water containing chloramines. Prime, by Seachem, is one product that claims to bind ammonia.

There are many variables to take in to account when choosing a method to acclimate new fish, including the number of fish that were put in a single transportation bag, the amount of water that was added to the bag, the size of the fish compared to the size of the bag and even when the fish ate its last meal can make it tricky to judge amounts of accumulated waste in a fish bag.

The most common methods of acclimation follow.

Methods to introducing fish to an aquarium:

Acclimation Method 1

1. Turn aquarium lights off while floating the fish.
2. Float the sealed bag with the fish inside on top of the aquarium water for 15 - 30 minutes. The salesperson should have filled at least half the bag with air, enabling the bag to float in your aquarium. Floating the fish bag on the surface of the aquarium allows the water in the bag to gradually change to the same temperature as the aquarium water.

Bag is left closed and floats on top of the water

3. Use a thermometer to ensure the temperature of the water in the fish bags is the same as the aquarium water.
4. Release the fish into the aquarium. To accomplish this, you can pinch the end of the bag and pour all of the water into a bucket, then pour the fish into the aquarium; OR pour the fish into a net over a sink or bucket to catch the water from the bag, and then release the fish into the aquarium. The key here is to keep store water from entering your aquarium.

CAUTION: Some fish such as angels and mandarins have spines which can get caught in a net.

CAUTION: Water from a fish store could contain copper or other medications! Do not add water from a fish bag to your aquarium!

Acclimation Method 2

   1. Turn aquarium lights off.

   2. Float sealed bag with the fish inside in the top of your aquarium or, if you prefer, in your sump for 15 minutes. The salesperson should have filled at least half the bag with air, enabling it to float in your aquarium. Floating the fish bag on the surface of the aquarium allows the water in the bag to gradually change to the same temperature as the water in the aquarium.

   3. Open the bag and roll down the sides to create an air pocket, which will allow the bag to continue to float.

Bag is open to add water (some fish jump, cover opening with a breathable material)

   4. Slowly add some water from your aquarium to the bag (about a 1/3 of the bag volume).

   5. After 10 minutes, repeat step 4. Do this two more times.

6. Release the fish into the aquarium. To release the fish you can pinch the end of the bag and pour all of the water into a bucket, then pour the fish into the aquarium; OR pour the fish into a net and then release the fish into the aquarium. The key here is to keep store water from entering your aquarium.

> *CAUTION: Fish such as angels and mandarins have spines which can get caught in a net.*

Acclimation Method 3

1. Turn off the aquarium light to avoid stressing the fish.
2. Float the sealed bag with the fish in the top of the aquarium or sump for 15 to 30 minutes. The salesperson should have filled at least half the bag with air, enabling the bag to float in your aquarium. This allows the water in the bag to gradually change to the same temperature as the aquarium water.
3. Put a clean nontoxic container or bucket in front of the aquarium. The number of fish and their sizes determine the size of the bucket. For two small fish (less than three inches each) a one gallon container will do.

> *NOTE: When acclimating a new fish make sure you keep it in a separate container from invertebrates and corals that you acclimate at the same time.*

4. Once the temperature of the new fish water is the same as your aquarium, open the bag and pour the fish gently into the bucket. If there is not enough water to cover the fish, place something under one side of the bucket to raise the water level on the other side.

Fish released into bucket of water

5. Add an ammonia neutralizing product to the bucket of water with the fish. There are several products available at fish stores used to quickly neutralize ammonia.

6. Start a siphon to slowly drip water from your aquarium into the container. The siphon is a section of airline tubing, generally four to six feet long, with an adjustable valve on one end.

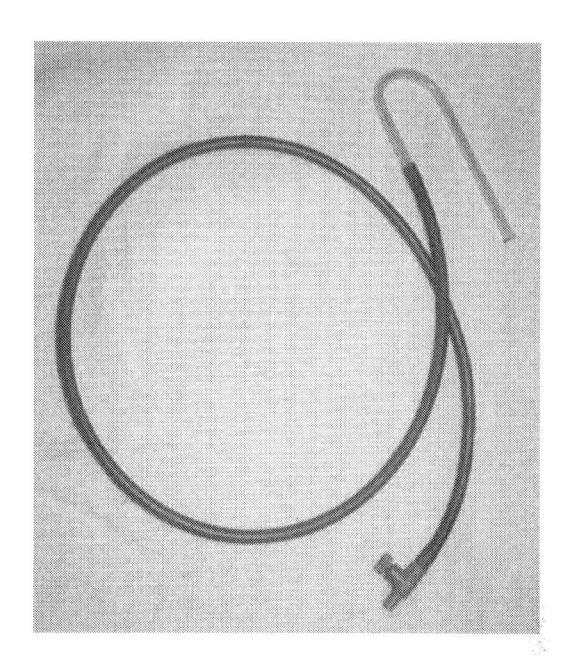

Drip line with plastic u-shape pipe to hang on rim of aquarium, airline tubing and valve

    Place the end of the tubing without the valve in your aquarium and suck on the valve end to begin water flowing. Place the valve end into the bucket and slowly open and close it until the valve allows just two to four drops per second to drip through.

Water from aquarium slowly dripping into bucket

7. Cover the bucket to keep fish from jumping out and to keep it dark.

8. When the water in the bucket has doubled, dip out half of the water and discard it.

9. Let the water level double again.

10. Now, transfer the fish one at a time to the aquarium using a fish net or small plastic container. Caution: Some fish, like angelfish and mandarin fish have rays which can get caught in a net.

NOTE: This unhurried acclimation method will slowly raise the pH along with leveling out specific gravity and other water parameters. Remember; always acclimate in a shaded or dark area as fish are sensitive to sudden light changes.

11. Add premixed saltwater to the aquarium to replace water removed for acclimation.

Whichever acclimation method you chose, follow these tips as well.

> *TIPS: Feed a small amount of food to help distract the original inhabitants from picking on the new fish. Leave aquarium light off for a few hours to calm fish and keep them from harassing each other. When new fish enter the aquarium, you may see both territorial disputes and changes in the pecking order. These behaviors are both natural.*

Chapter 8

Invertebrates are Beneficial and Fun

Invertebrates are entertaining with their playful antics, daily routines and unique personalities. Snails, crabs, urchins, starfish, fan worms, and shrimps are all invertebrates; these animals do not have a backbone. Some of these animals are actually beneficial additions for a saltwater aquarium because they consume unwanted algae, detritus (particles of organic material) and uneaten fish foods. Others are simply fun to watch.

It takes a bit of knowledge to know which fish will live with invertebrates and there is a large group of invertebrates which are safe to be mixed with most fish and corals. Generally you will find that the fish are the aggressors and will attack and consume invertebrates. As many humans enjoy the delicious taste of shrimp, so do many predatory fish.

After your aquarium has cycled, the live rock will appear clean and empty. Organisms like plants, algae, bacteria, etc., will soon cover the once pristine rock. As livestock is added and fed, waste levels begin to build; these levels are naturally reduced to nitrate, a food for algae. Nitrate, combined with aquarium and ambient light, provides perfect conditions for algae to grow. There is actually a purpose for this unsightly algae - it helps reduce nitrate levels. The trick is to control algae, not eliminate it, and we do this with a carefully-selected balance of fish and invertebrates.

In this section we will discuss different types of invertebrates and how they interact in an aquarium. Invertebrates are sold individually or in assortments called reef cleaners, cleaning packs or cleanup crews. These packages include snails, crabs, shrimp, etc.

If your rock is clean, it will take few invertebrates to keep it clean. Obviously, add more invertebrates if your rocks have excessive algae growth or detritus build up. Invertebrates can be added at any time.

Some invertebrates, like sea anemones, require special lighting and will not live long with the simple light systems in most basic saltwater setups.

Invertebrates are extremely sensitive to rapid changes in water quality. Because of this, it is important to use a proven method to acclimate new invertebrates into your aquarium. (See the section "Bringing Your New Invertebrates Home".) To keep water quality ideal and nitrate levels less than 10ppm, it is important to schedule and implement consistent partial water changes. (See "How to Care for Your Aquarium", Chapter 11.) Many medications to treat fish will kill invertebrates like copper. Before treating your aquarium always read medication and additive labels.

While there is an enormous selection of invertebrates available to hobbyists, we will limit our discussion to hardy, easy to keep invertebrates that are most beneficial to a saltwater aquarium.

Anemone

Bubble Tip Anemone (Entacmaea quadricolor), Long Tentacle Anemone (Macrodactyla doreensis), and Pink Tipped Haitian Reef Anemone (Condylactis sp.)

Bubble Tip and Long Tentacle Anemones

Anemones' tubular or flat-shaped bodies are covered with harmless looking tentacles which flow gracefully in water currents.

These tentacles are coated with stinging cells (nematocysts) which are used to paralyze small swimming animals. Tentacles are also used to push food towards the anemone's mouth.

Anemones attach themselves to rocks, sides of the aquarium or anywhere else they desire. While you can place your star anemone in an optimal location in your aquarium so that it looks spectacular, there is only an off-chance that your pet will stay put. There is a better chance that, when you least expect it, your prized anemone will select another, less optimal spot. Sometimes an anemone will move itself and will still be visible; other times it will attach itself totally out of view, behind rockwork. Sadly, some errant anemones have been known to fasten themselves beside gorgeous and expensive corals in a rather unfriendly fashion. Your prized coral, being unable to move, can be stung to death!

Often, while the anemone slithers along looking for its perfect location, it will sting and damage corals along the way. It is not easy to move an anemone once it attaches to a rock; more often than not you can end up tearing its flesh to get it free. For these reasons, it is preferable to keep anemones in aquariums that do not contain corals.

Anemones are similar to coral in that they both have symbiotic algae (zooxanthellae) living within their tissue which, through photosynthesis, creates nutrients (carbohydrates) for these animals. Bright light is a must when keeping these creatures, with a specific spectrum in order for photosynthesis to take place. Anemones get most of their nutrients from zooxanthellae in their tissue, however regular feeding (every week to every other week) is beneficial. Feed them meaty foods such as eat silversides (small whole fish) and chopped raw seafood like squid, krill, shrimp and fish.

When anemones feel threatened or need to expel waste, they will deflate their tentacles and bodies. Good water quality is essential for optimum health and will allow them to grow to their full size, which in some species can be quite large.

If you are an experienced hobbyist and desire to own a large beautiful anemone, consider Green Carpet (Stichodactyla haddoni), which can grow up to three feet across. This anemone generally lives on the sandy bottom and usually attaches its foot to the bottom of the aquarium as shown in the picture below. Green Carpet Anemones look amazing displayed in large aquariums; these animals have a few special requirements that will ensure that they, and their tank mates, remain content.

Green Carpet Anemone 18" across

Anemones are well known for their symbiotic relationship with clownfish. Most of us have seen pictures of Clownfish hiding or playing in the tentacles of a sea anemone.

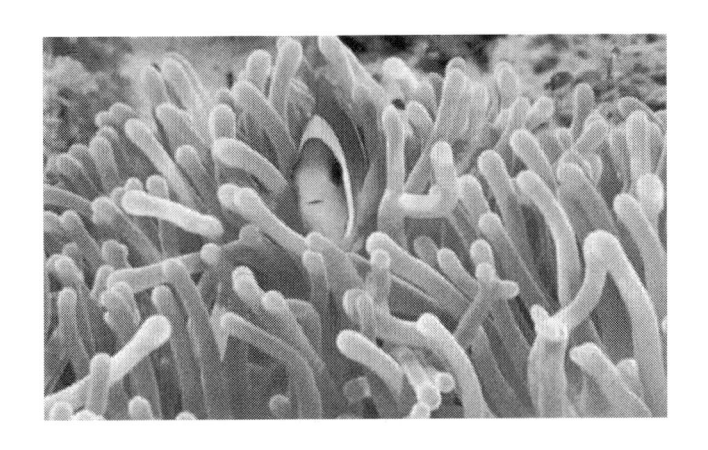

Clownfish relaxing in its Anemone

Clownfish will hide in an anemone for protection and will, in return, share food with the anemone. Some anemones such as the Pink Tipped Haitian Reef will not normally host clownfish, while Bubble Tip Anemones make great hosts. Clownfish which can typically be found in Bubble Tips include Clarkii Clownfish (Amphiprion clarkii), Maroon Clownfish (Premnas biaculeatus), Ocellaris Clownfish (Amphiprion ocellaris), Tomato Clownfish (Amphiprion frenatus) and True Percula Clownfish (Amphiprion percula).

Crabs

In order for a crab to grow it must periodically shed its exoskeleton (external skeleton) which supports and protects its body. An exoskeleton which has been shed has incredible detail and often looks like a dead crab lying on the sand. Before being alarmed, remove the remains and, if it is empty, you will find that it is simply an exoskeleton.

Hermit Crabs are different from true crabs as they do not make their own shells. Hermit crabs use empty snail shells to house and protect their bodies from predators. As they grow, they seek out larger shells so it is sensible to offer different sized empty shells in the aquarium. If a Hermit Crab does not find the right sized empty shell, it can drag a snail out of its shell killing it.

Arrow Crab (Stenorhynchus seticornis)

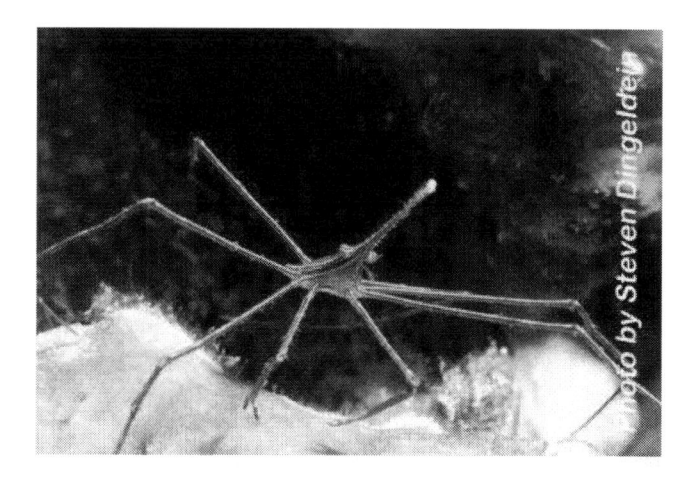

Arrow Crab

An Arrow Crab has long spindly legs with a narrow body and a long pointed head. It is also called a spider crab. This crab will crawl on rocks and sand in search of food. At feeding, an Arrow Crab will literally run across an aquarium to grab a chunk of food. It is territorial and will fight off fish and invertebrates to protect its food.

Arrow Crabs are very hardy and can grow to over six inches in length from leg to leg. Only keep one Arrow Crab in aquariums less than 55 gallons. They are beneficial carnivores, great scavengers of meaty food and will eat nuisance worms such as Bristleworms. They are a fun, unique crab to watch.

CAUTION: Add this crab to your reef only if you have a problem with bristleworms!

Arrow Crabs may eat Xenia, feather dusters, coral polyps and attack other crabs and shrimp. It is nocturnal and can harm fish at night.

Blue Leg Reef Hermit Crabs (Calcinus tricolor)

Blue Leg Hermit Crab

Blue Leg Hermit Crabs are peaceful and excellent reef cleaners. Their legs are bright blue with a few red bands. While Blue Leg Hermits stay small, their voracious appetite for nuisance algae, detritus and excess food makes them perfect reef scavengers. Only growing to an inch long allows this crab to squeeze into and clean tight spaces in the rockwork where other larger scavengers cannot reach. They will also sift through sand searching for food.

Blue Leg Hermit Crabs eat many types of algae including hair algae, film algae, cyanobacteria (red slime algae) and detritus. Their small size makes them a great addition to the cleanup crew. Add one Blue Leg Hermit for each five to ten gallons of aquarium water.

They are safe with corals. As the crab grows, keep various sized empty shells in aquarium; remember that it can pull small snails out of their shells.

Decorator Crab (Camposcia retusa)

Decorator Crab with yellow and pink sponge stuck to its body and leg

    Decorator crabs appear a bit zany, to say the least. These strange creatures attach sponge, small shells, coral polyps, plants, algae and other sea debris of their choosing to their legs and body as camouflage. This is a survival technique that can be a lifesaver in the ocean and is fun to watch in an aquarium- unless your crab begins tearing off pieces of your prized soft coral or Zoanthid polyp.
    This crab is easy to keep, grows up to four inches across and requires plenty of hiding places to feel secure. Decorator crabs can be found at night scavenging the sand and live rock for uneaten meaty foods. If necessary, their diet can be supplemented with mysis shrimp and other prepared meaty fish foods.

Emerald Crab (Mithraculus sculptus)

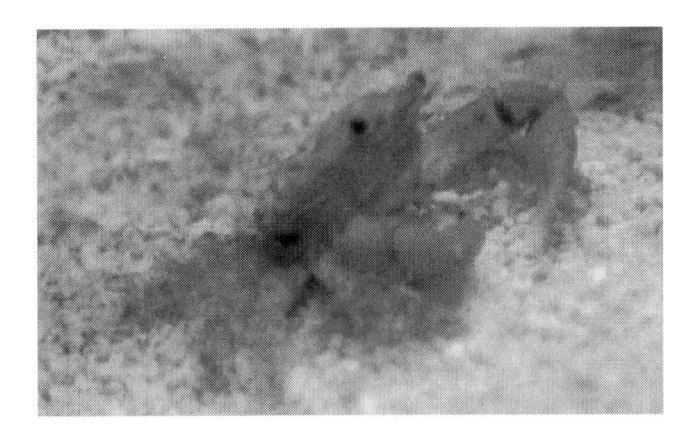

Emerald Crab

Emerald Crabs are green, with a flat shaped body, hairy legs and large claws. They use their claws to scrape and eat micro and macro algae (including bubble algae) off the rock.

Even though Emerald Crabs are nocturnal, once they are used to their new environment they will be out during the day scouring rocks for food. As long as an Emerald Crab has plenty of food, it is safe with corals and other invertebrates. These creatures are omnivorous and opportunistic; when hungry, they will turn their attention to fish, corals and other invertebrates. Luckily most reefs create a constant supply of food, so this is rarely a cause for concern. If your reef is too clean, supplement with meaty fish foods and algae sheets.

Emerald Crabs grow to two and a half inches long. They are territorial towards their own species, so keep only one Emerald Crab per 40 pounds of live rock.

Halloween Hermit Crab (Ciliopagurus strigatus)

Halloween Hermit Crab

The colorful Halloween Hermit Crab has brilliant red legs with bright orange bands. These crabs will eat hair algae, cyanobacteria, detritus and uneaten food. Halloween Hermits will also sift through sand looking for food.

Halloween Hermit Crabs grow large, about two inches long, and their shells can knock down loose corals and small rocks. They are relatively peaceful and safe with corals and other invertebrates. As the crab grows, keep various sized empty shells in aquarium; remember that it can pull snails out of their shells.

Red Tip Hermit Crab (Clibanarius sp.)

Red Tip Hermit Crabs

Red Tip Hermit Crabs also known as Red Leg Hermit Crabs are small, peaceful and very similar to Blue Leg Crabs. Growing to a scant inch long allows it to clean in tight places. It has a great appetite for nuisance algae, including green hair and cyanobacteria.

Red Tip Hermit Crabs are safe for corals and most other invertebrates; they may attack snails for their shells.

Red Tip Hermit crabs are omnivores. If food is scarce, feed these crabs Nori algae sheets.

Scarlet Reef Hermit Crab (Paguristes cadenati)

Scarlet Reef Hermit Crab

Scarlet Reef Hermit Crabs are very hardy and some of the best choices for a reef aquarium. Easy to recognize with its bright red legs and a red body, Scarlet Reef Hermit Crabs spend their lives searching and eating nuisance filamentous algae, red cyanobacteria and detritus.

The Scarlet Reef Hermit Crab will only grow to one and a half inches in length. This crab is safe with corals and most invertebrates. On occasional they are known to attack snails for their shells. They are peaceful with tank mates and their own kind.

They are omnivores and will eat excess fish foods and Nori seaweed or any food that is high in spirulina, kelp and other forms of algae.

Zebra Hermit Crab (Calcinus laevimanus)

Zebra Hermit Crab

A Zebra Hermit Crab is a great choice for a mini reef. It gets its name from the black and white bands on its legs and pinchers. Also known as the Left Handed Hermit Crab, this crab will withdraw into its shell for protection and use its large left claw to block the entrance.

Zebra Hermit Crabs are great scavengers with voracious appetites for filamentous algae like green hair algae, cyanobacteria (red slime algae) and detritus.

NOTE: They are one of the few true herbivore crabs.

If food is scarce, feed these crabs Nori algae sheets.

Although they are peaceful and reef safe, they will attack and kill snails for their shells.

Fan Worms

Feather Dusters look like a cluster of feathers sticking out of a tube. A worm creates this soft, flexible tube around its body for protection. The feathery part that sticks out of the tube is called the crown or fan, and at its base is the worm's mouth.

When a Feather Duster is frightened or concerned it will quickly pull its crown into its tube for protection. If highly stressed, it may even shed its crown; it will usually grow a new one.

In a reef aquarium, gently bury the Feather Duster's tube under the sand so that the crown is pointing upward into light current. At feeding time the Feather Duster will spread its crown to capture food floating in the water. Captured food is moved by cilia (hair-like motile projection) down a groove to the mouth. This filter feeder eats phytoplankton as well as fine detritus from the water. There are also many prepared liquid and frozen foods for filter feeders.

Reef aquariums stocked with numerous filter feeders may want to feed daily. If there are few filter feeders in the reef, feed them just a few times a week. A turkey baster may be used to lightly blow food into the current moving towards the crown. If you try to blow food directly at the crown it will retract into its tube.

Feather Dusters are hardy, easy to keep and peaceful with their tank mates. They are safe with corals and other invertebrates.

Hawaiian Feather Duster (Sabellastarte sp.)

Feather Dusters

Also called the Giant Feather Duster, Hawaiian Feather Dusters can grow up to seven inches long with a crown reaching seven inches in diameter. The crown can be tan with dark brown bands or tan or brown with white bands. These earthy colors do not make them sound exciting but they add a beauty and unique oddity to a reef.

Dwarf Feather Duster (Bispira sp.)

Dwarf Feather Duster

This animal can grow up to four inches long. The tube is a light brown color and the crown can be red and white, pink and white, lime green, white and yellow.

Coco Worm (Protula bispiralis)

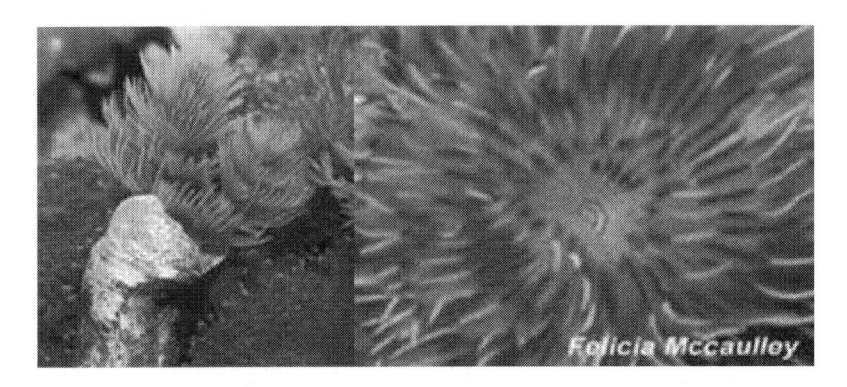

Coco Worm and close up of a red and white crown

Coco Worms are unique among fan worms because they secrete a hard calcium carbonate protective tube around their bodies. Sticking out of the open end of the tube is a beautiful crown with feathery rays in shades of pink, yellow, red, orange or white or some combination of these colors.

Coco Worms create a hard, calcareous tube up to 24 inches long with interesting bends or spirals delineated along its length. When frightened or concerned this worm will quickly pull its filter feeding crown into its tube for protection.

Feather-shaped rays of the crown are used to collect food from water. Cilia move food particles down the ray to the mouth of the worm. Coco worms do not have a trap door (operculum) at the open end of the tube to keep the air out if lifted out of the water. When transporting this creature, fill a fish bag with aquarium water and place the coco worm in the bag taking care to keep it totally submersed.

Place the Coco Worm in a shaded place in the rockwork or on the sand. If placed on the sand, gently bury its tube under the sand so its crown is pointing upward, or place it in a hole or crevice in the rockwork where the crown receives light current.

These filter feeders eat phytoplankton, zooplankton, bacteria, and even fine detritus floating in the water. Supplement their natural diet with prepared liquid and frozen foods that contain phytoplankton and zooplankton. In a well-stocked reef with other filter feeders, you can feed daily; if you have a few filter feeders, feed them only a few times a week. A turkey baster may be used to lightly blow food into the current towards the crown. If you try to blow food directly at the crown it will retract into its tube and will not eat.

Like stony corals, the Coco Worm requires calcium carbonate to grow its calcareous tube, so be sure to add calcium and carbonate to a reef housing this creature.

Coco Worms are safe with all corals and invertebrates, but some crabs may pester the Coco Worm, causing it to retract. If a crab persistently bothers a Coco Worm such that its crown is retracted the majority of the time, it is time to remove the crab.

Sea Stars

Brittle Star and Serpent Star

Harlequin Serpent Star

There are up to 2000 species of starfish documented but few are considered reef-safe. The majority of Brittle Stars and Serpent Stars *are* considered reef safe.

Brittle Stars and Serpent Stars usually spend their days hiding in the rockwork or sand below it. This type of starfish will normally stay in the shelter of the rocks and reach its arms out to grab meaty foods drifting by, pulling the food back to its mouth. Brittle Stars and Serpent Stars are carnivores, making them excellent scavengers of detritus and uneaten fish food.

These starfish will burrow into the sand and move around helping to keep the sand substrate oxygenated.

Starfish in this family stay small and medium size and are safe with corals and other invertebrates. Larger stars such as a Green Brittle Star can capture and eat fish and motile invertebrates like hermit crabs.

Chocolate Chip Sea Star (Protoreaster nodosus)

Chocolate Chip Sea Star

Chocolate Sea Stars are hardy, easy to care for and are a smart addition to FOWLR (Fish Only with Live Rock) aquariums. This sea star has protective dark pointy horns called tubercles on top of its body and arms which resemble chocolate chips.

This sea star grows large, up to 16" in diameter. Since it is easy to catch and remove from most aquariums it can be raised in smaller aquariums and moved to a larger one if required. This sea star should be kept in aquarium with passive non-predatory fish. Large Angelfish, puffers and triggerfish may pick on or attack this sea star.

Chocolate Sea Stars will cruise across the glass, rocks and sand looking for meaty leftover food. This sea star is not reef safe as it can eat clams, zoanthid polyps, sponges and other sessile invertebrates. Their diet can be supplemented with chopped clam, shrimp, and prepared meaty seafood.

Red Knob Sea Star, African (Protoreaster linckii)

Red Knob Sea Star

The Red Knob Sea Star is unusual with its deep red tubercles (protective pointy horns) running across the top of its meaty grayish body and arms. The red nodules are joined by a series of low running red ridges creating a beautiful interconnected pattern on the top of the back and arms.

Caring for this sea star is much like that of a Chocolate Chip Sea Star; once acclimated to an aquarium, it is a hardy addition. Most death occurs from shipping and/or improper acclimation. Red Knob Sea Stars can grow up to a foot in diameter.

Keep Red Knob Sea Star in a large FOWLR (Fish Only with Live Rock) aquarium with nonaggressive fish. It should not be mixed with large angelfish or butterfly fish which may nip, or triggerfish and puffers for which may become a meal.

This sea star is a great scavenger and readily searches for uneaten fish food. It is not reef safe as will consume clams, Zoanthid polyps, sponges, tube worms, sea anemones, sea stars and other sessile invertebrates. Their diet can be supplemented with chopped clam, scallop, shrimp, and prepared meaty seafood.

Sand Sifting Sea Star (Astropecten polycanthus)

Sand Sifting Sea Star

Sand Sifting Sea Star makes a great addition to a reef's clean-up crew. They are peaceful and help keep the sand clean.

This star burrows into the sand in a most interesting manner (they appear to slowly vanish) in search of food, thus oxygenating the sand. When an aquarium is setup, the sand in the bottom of the aquarium is white or light tan. Over time, algae, detritus, bacteria, etc. grow on the sand making it dark and dingy. Servicing the reef by vacuuming the gravel while changing part of the water will help clean this up, but the sand will slowly start turning dark again. A Sand Sifting Sea Star 'churns' the sand, giving it a cleaner appearance.

Sand Sifting Sea Stars are omnivores. They eat detritus, small crustacean, microfauna (microscopic animals) and uneaten foods. They are most active at night after the lights go out. In a large, established reef there may be enough food for the starfish. In cleaner aquariums it is best to supplement their diet with a small amount of fish food such as mysis shrimp. Feed them at night when the fish are resting. One Sand Sifting Sea Star can usually keep the sand in a 90 gallon tank clean.

Sand Sifting Sea Star is peaceful and grow to around six inches in an aquarium and up to eight inches or larger in the ocean. This Sea Star is safe with corals, but like most starfish, they can eat small bivalves like clams and urchins and shrimp.

Shrimp

Shrimp, like crabs, periodically molt their external skeleton (exoskeleton) to grow. A shrimp may hide for several days while its new exoskeleton hardens. When they shed their exoskeleton it will look identical to the shrimp including the antennas, except it will be hollow. When you see it lying on the bottom of the aquarium and it is empty it means your shrimp now has a pretty new and slightly larger exoskeleton.

Banded Coral Shrimp (Stenopus hispidus)

Banded Coral Shrimp

The Banded Coral Shrimp has an attractive red and white stripped pattern, is easy to keep and is often reasonably priced. These facts make them popular among saltwater and reef aquariums keepers.

While they often hide during the day and are active at night or when food is added to the aquarium, these striking shrimp are great scavengers, searching through the rock and sand looking for uneaten meaty foods and other detritus. They will also eat pesky bristle worms.

At up to 3" body length and another 3" of antennae, the Banded Coral Shrimp is one of the larger aquarium shrimp. Keep mated pairs or keep this shrimp by itself; it should not be kept with other species of shrimp since it can harass and even kill them.

Blood Red Fire Shrimp (Lysmata debelius)

Blood Red Fire Shrimp

Fire Shrimp are very striking with their deep red body with white dots, long white antennae and white front legs. This cleaner shrimp uses its long white antennas to attract fish swimming by that want to be cleaned.

Fire Shrimp grow to about two inches long and spend most of their time hanging upside down in their favorites spot in a cave or under a ledge. They are more likely to remain hidden among the rock work than Scarlet Skunk Cleaner Shrimp which are usually out in the open. Fire shrimp can be kept individually, in pair or in a group. They also mix well with other shrimp.

At feeding time, Fire Shrimp will dart of their hiding place, run after and grab bits of meaty foods and retreat.

Like other cleaner shrimp, Fire Shrimp can set up a "cleaning station" in a mini reef. They actually pick parasites and dead tissue off their fishy tank mates. A fish will come to the cleaning station and hold its body close to the shrimp so it can climb on. Besides cleaning its body, this shrimp can also do dental work, cleaning inside the mouth of the fish.

Fire Shrimp are hardy once established in a reef. They are safe with corals and invertebrates.

Candy Stripe Pistol Shrimp (Alpheus randalli) and Tiger Snapping Shrimp (Alpheus bellulus)

Look closely; the Candy Stripe Pistol Shrimp is at the bottom of Yasha White Ray Shrimp Goby

The Pistol or Snapping Shrimp get their name by the cracking sound that their powerful, enlarged claw makes when it quickly closes. Candy Stripe Pistol Shrimp and Tiger Snapping Shrimp are two of the most commonly kept species.

Candy Stripe Pistol Shrimp, as its name suggests, is a pretty shrimp with red and white alternating stripes. A Tiger Snapping Shrimp is drab in comparison with its tan body and dark bands. Candy Stripe Pistol Shrimp will grow to about 2 inches long while the Tiger Snapping Shrimp grows larger up to three inches.

One of the most captivating characteristics about some Pistol Shrimp is their symbiotic relationship with Gobies. A Pistol Shrimp and Goby will live together in a burrow which the shrimp excavated. The shrimp will maintain the burrow while the Goby stands guard near the entrance. When a predator comes near, the Goby alerts the Pistol Shrimp. They both hide in the burrow until the danger is gone. They will also sleep together in their burrow. A few Gobies that will pair up with Candy Stripe Pistol Shrimp and Tiger Snapping Shrimp are the Hi Fin Red Banded Goby, Yasha White Ray Shrimp Goby and Yellow Watchman Goby.

NOTE: Not all Pistol Shrimps will team up with a goby.

Make sure the sand is at least one and a half inches deep for these shrimp to make their burrow. When adding a Pistol Shrimp to a reef you do not know where he will build his burrow.

These shrimp are carnivorous scavengers eating any meaty food that comes near its burrow.

Pistol shrimp are safe with corals and most invertebrates, but can eat shrimp smaller than themselves.

Peppermint Shrimp (Lysmata wurdemanni)

Peppermint Shrimp

Peppermint Shrimp are small, easy to care for and can be beneficial in a mini reef. They are inexpensive compared to some of the more colorful shrimp.

Peppermint Shrimp are hardy and grow to two inches long. They can be red or a light pink with dark red stripes and bands on its body. Add one Peppermint Shrimp or add a group of them, they will get along together. They also live well with other peaceful shrimp.

Peppermint Shrimp generally hide in the rockwork during the day and run out at feeding time. They are most active during the night and you can watch their activities with moonlights (a few blue LED lights). They will venture over the entire aquarium looking for food.

They are great eaters of meaty food and detritus. Given the chance they will steal food from corals and anemones. To feed corals it is a good practice to put food for the shrimp at the opposite end of the aquarium before attempting to target-feed corals.

The Peppermint Shrimp is highly sought after for its ability to eat nuisance aiptasia or glass anemones. They are several species sold under the trade name Peppermint Shrimp, but choose only shrimp collected from the Atlantic and gulf coast region if you want them to chow down on aiptasia.

Peppermint shrimp are generally reef safe, but they will occasionally aggravate corals by ripping food out of coral polyps.

Scarlet Skunk Cleaner Shrimp (Lysmata amboinensis)

Scarlet Skunk Cleaner Shrimp

The Scarlet Skunk Cleaner Shrimp is one of my personal favorites. It is easy to identify with two red stripes and one white stripe in the middle going down its back. It has long white antennas that are used to attract fish that need a cleaner shrimp.

Scarlet Skunk Cleaner Shrimp are peaceful, hardy and easy to keep. They only grow to two inches in length but when you see the adults they look much larger because of their long antennas. Keep one or several together in a reef. Unlike Fire Shrimp, Scarlet Skunk Cleaner Shrimp will stay out in the open. Both of these shrimp will live in the same aquarium but will stay in different spots among the rocks.

This Cleaner Shrimp can set up a "cleaning station" in a mini reef where they will pick parasites and dead tissue off fish tank mates. A fish will come to the cleaning station and hold its body close to the shrimp so it can climb on. The fish will stay in the cleaning station area while the shrimp cleans it body. Cleaner shrimp will remove and eat Ich, a common parasite that attaches to saltwater fish. It can also perform dental cleaning inside the mouth of the fish.

They are carnivores and greedily nab any meaty food that enters the aquarium. At feeding time it can swim into the water column and compete with peaceful fish for food.

Scarlet Skunk Cleaner Shrimp are safe with corals and invertebrates. The only downside is this shrimp may try to steal food from corals which you are target feeding. In this case, feed these shrimp well before feeding corals.

Spotted Cleaner Shrimp (Periclimenes yucatanicus)

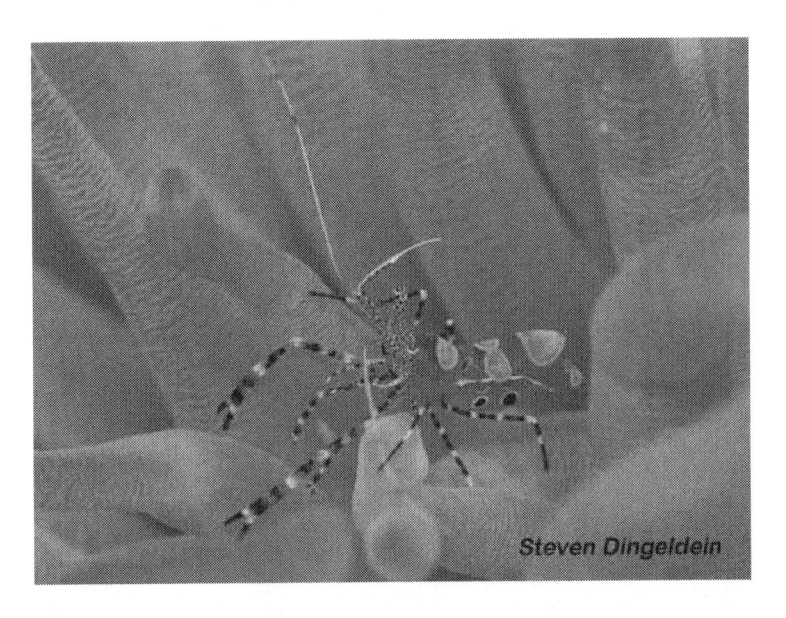

Spotted Cleaner Shrimp

The Spotted Cleaner Shrimp has a transparent body with white spots on its back and tail and blue to lavender markings on their abdomen and legs. They are usually found in the Caribbean hiding amongst the tentacles of Condylactus Sea Anemones.

This shrimp is peaceful, stays small growing to an inch long and, like clownfish, uses sea anemones for protection. Keep this cute little shrimp with small nonaggressive fish. It will venture outside the anemone to grab food if kept with small passive fish, eating meaty foods. In the wild, this striking shrimp will its antennae to attract fish so that it can clean (eat) parasites off their scales. It may continue this exercise in the home aquarium.

Snails

Astraea Snail (Astraea tecta)

Astraea Snail

The Astraea Snail has a unique pyramid-shaped spiral shell with grooves along the outer perimeter. These snails are peaceful, easy to keep and grow to about an inch long.

Astraeas are herbivores that consume film algae such as diatoms, short filamentous algae and cyanobacteria off the rock work. They will also clean algae off the walls of the aquarium.

While safe to mix with corals and other invertebrates, this snail cannot turn itself over in the sand. It needs either a rock or side of the aquarium to grip onto to upright itself. When introducing an Astraea Snail to an aquarium, make sure to turn the shell such that its opening is on the sand or rock. If you notice a snail is on its back, turn the shell. If left upside down they will eventually die or become food for other tank inhabitants such as a hermits crab.

Add one Astraea Snail for each 10 gallons of water; supplement feed with dried Nori seaweed or a food that is high in spirulina, kelp and other forms of algae.

Banded Trochus Snail (Trochus sp.)

Banded Trochus Snail

Banded Trochus Snails are some of the best snails for the reef. They are peaceful, easy to keep and have a distinctive pyramid-shaped shell.

This snail is an herbivore with a voracious appetite for film algae, cyanobacteria, and diatoms on live rock, sand, and sides of the aquarium.

Banded Trochus Snails grow to an inch high. Its pyramid shape shell makes it unlikely to knock down rocks or corals from the rockwork. They spend most of the day hiding and come out to eat in the dark.

One benefit to keeping Banded Trochus Snails in a reef aquarium is that they may actually breed and populate the reef. They can also turn themselves over if they happen to fall, unlike Astraea and Mexican Turbo Snails that simply lay there and die or get eaten by crabs.

Banded Trochus Snails are safe with corals and other invertebrates.

Cerith Snail (Cerithium sp.)

Cerith Snails

Cerith Snails are ideal for a reef aquarium given their diverse appetite. They have a small conical shaped shell and grow to a little over an inch long. They can fit into and clean tight places in rocks and within coral polyps.

These snails consume detritus, uneaten food, film algae, hair algae, cyanobacteria and diatoms in the sand, on the rocks and attached to the sides of the aquarium. Cerith Snails are nocturnal and may not be very active during the day. They are hardy, peaceful and you may find them buried in the sand.

Cerith Snails are safe with corals and other invertebrates. Their small size and varied tastes makes them a great addition to a cleaning crew. Add one per ten gallons of aquarium water.

Mexican Turbo Snail (Turbo fluctuosa)

Mexican Turbo Snail

The Mexican Turbo Snail is one of the larger snails and gets its name from its thick turban-shaped shell.

The Mexican Turbo Snail is peaceful, easy to keep and grows to over two inches. Mexican Turbo Snails are herbivores and voraciously eat nuisance micro algae, filamentous algae like green and red hair algae and diatoms off rockwork and sides of aquarium. While searching for food their large shells can knock down loose rocks and corals.

A Mexican Turbo Snail is safe with corals and other invertebrates. This snail cannot turn itself over in the sand. It needs either a rock or side of the aquarium to grip and upright itself. When introducing a Mexican Turbo Snail into an aquarium, turn its shell such that the opening is on the sand. If left upside down this snail will eventually die and be eaten by other tank inhabitants such as a hermits crab.

Mexican Turbo Snails are good additions to the cleanup crew. Add one snail per every 20 to 40 gallons of water. Adding a few at a time ensures they have an ongoing food source. If the food becomes limited, feed them dried Nori seaweed or a food that is high in spirulina, kelp and other forms of algae.

Nassarius Snail (Nassarius sp.)

Nassarius Snail

Nassarius Snails are excellent for a reef aquarium because they help keep the sand clean, stirred and oxygenated.

The most exciting feature about Nassarius Snails takes place during feeding. Nassarius Snails spend most of their time under the sand, usually with their proboscis (long flexible tube) sticking above the sand to alert them when food is present. As soon as it senses food in the aquarium it quickly emerges from the sand. It is neat to watch numerous Nassarius Snails emerge from the sand at the same time, reminiscent of an old horror movie where the living dead rise from their graves.

Nassarius Snails from Tonga are some of the largest and hardiest snails available, growing up to an inch long. Nassarius Snails glide across the sand and glass at record snail speeds.

Nassarius Snails are carnivores and thrive on uneaten meaty foods, detritus and fish waste. They are safe with corals and other invertebrates. Nassarius Snails should be part of the cleanup crew.

Nerite Snail (Nerita sp.)

Nerite Snail

A Nerite Snail is a great small scavenger with a rounded shell. The Caribbean variety has a pretty black and white wavy zebra-like pattern on its shell.

Nerite Snails are herbivores that eat detritus, film and hair algae, diatoms and cyanobacteria. These snails do a great job of cleaning the rock work and walls of an aquarium.

The Nerite Snail is peaceful, easy to keep and grow to about an inch long. Their small size and smooth shells generally keep them for knocking down loose rocks or corals. Nerite Snails tend to be active at night.

Nerite Snails are voracious algae eaters and, if needed, their diet can be supplemented with Nori seaweed or a food that is high in spirulina, kelp and other forms of algae.

Nerite Snails are safe with corals and invertebrates. Add one snail for each 10 gallons of aquarium water.

Sea Urchins

Pencil Urchin (Eucidaris tribuloides)

Beautiful Pencil Urchin

Pin Cushion Urchin (Lytechinus vaniegatus)

Pin Cushion Urchin

Sea Urchins have a spherical or oval shape shell covered with spines for protection. Sea Urchins are found in a variety of colors including purple, red, brown, black and light pink.

Sea Urchins usually stay in one place during the day and are active at night. Most sea urchins like Pencil and Pincushion are great at eating many types of algae including coralline algae. Coralline algae will grow on rocks, encrusting them in a pleasant pink or purple color. It is beneficial since its hard calcium structure keeps some algae from taking hold and growing on live rock. If you like the way coraline algae looks, then limit the number of urchins you keep.

If you have a bad nuisance algae problem you can add several Urchins since they are relatively easy to catch and remove once algae is under control. They are not recommended for most reef aquariums and use caution when kept with rock work. They are bulldozers that can knock down substantial size rocks and corals as they munch along.

Besides knocking things down they can eat and damage certain corals. Several species of urchins will try to protect themselves from predators by sticking pieces of algae, shells, pebbles, loose frags (small corals), zooanthid colonies onto their spines. Some Urchins will eat coral polyps.

You typically do not need an urchin to control algae on live rock and it is safer to use crabs and snails. If you still choose to add a sea urchin, the Blue Tuxedo Urchin (Mespilia globulus) is one of the best choices.

Blue Tuxedo Urchin (Mespilia globulus)

Blue Tuxedo Urchin

Blue Tuxedo Urchin has short spines and blue bands without spines. It does a great job eating algae and may eat beneficial coraline algae. They are easy to keep and grow up to three inches long.

Like other urchins, the Blue Tuxedo is up at night foraging for algae and uneaten food on rocks, sand and sides of aquarium and rest during the day. They have very sharp spines so take care when handling or transporting them. If you keep zooanthid colonies in your reef, Blue Tuxedo Urchin may pull them loose and carry them around as camouflage along with, algae, shells etc.

Bringing Your New Invertebrates Home

Acclimation Method

1. Turn off the aquarium light to avoid stressing the invertebrates.
2. Float the sealed bag with the invertebrates inside the aquarium or sump water for 15 to 30 minutes. The salesperson should have filled at least half the bag with air, enabling the bag to float in your aquarium. Floating the bag allows the water in the bag to gradually change to the same temperature as the aquarium water.
3. Put a clean, nontoxic or food-grade container or bucket in front of the aquarium. The number and size of the invertebrates you are adding to your aquarium determines the size of the bucket you will need. For twelve small snails, for example, a one gallon container will do.

NOTE: When acclimating new invertebrates make sure you keep it in a separate container from fish and corals that you acclimate at the same time.

4. Once the temperature of the water in the plastic bag is the same as the water in the aquarium, open the bag and pour the inverts gently into the bucket. If there is not enough water to cover the invertebrates, place something under one side of the bucket to make a pocket of deep water inside.

Invertebrates released into bucket of water

NOTE: This slow acclimation method will slowly raise the pH as well as level out other water parameters including specific gravity.

    5. Add an ammonia neutralizing product to the bucket of water with the invertebrates. There are several products available at aquarium stores which will quickly neutralize ammonia.

    6. Start a siphon to slowly drip water from your aquarium into the container. The siphon is a section of airline tubing generally four to six feet long with an adjustable valve on one end.

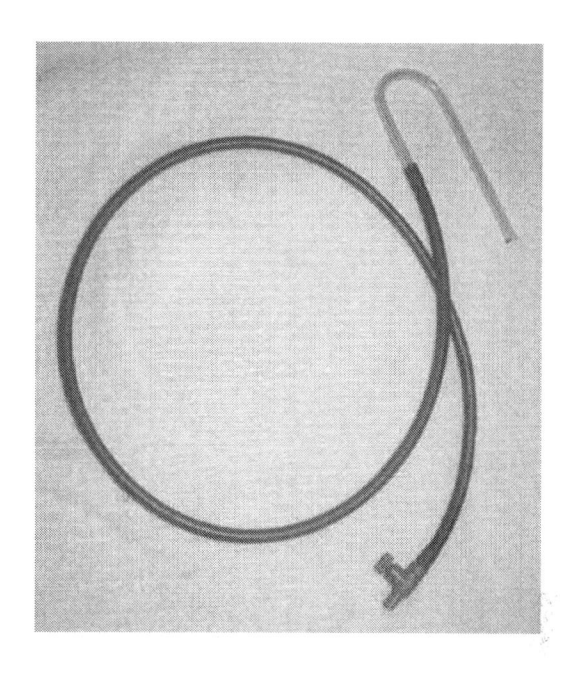

Drip line with plastic u-shape pipe to hang on rim of aquarium, airline tubing and valve

Place the end of the tubing without the valve in your aquarium or sump if it is high enough off the ground to create a flow; then suck on the valve end to begin water flow. Place the tubing in the bucket and slowly open and close the valve until it drips two to four drops per second.

Water from aquarium slowly dripping into bucket

7. Cover the bucket to keep invertebrates like snails from climbing out and to keep the drip bucket dark.
8. When the water in the bucket has doubled, dip out about half of the water and discard.
9. Let the water level double again.
10. Test the pH of the water in the bucket. If it matches the water of the aquarium acclimation is complete. If not continue the drip method until pH of the bucket matches your reef.
11. Next, transfer the invertebrates to the aquarium using a fish net or small plastic container.

NOTE: Make sure all snails are turned so the shell opening is against the sand or rock.

CAUTION: DO NOT add water from the fish bag to your aquarium as this water will most likely have different parameters than your aquarium. Fish stores may have also added medication to their water, so it is sensible to simply throw that water away.

12. Add premixed saltwater to the aquarium to replace water just removed for acclimation.

TIPS: Feed a small amount of food to help distract the original tank inhabitants from picking on the new invertebrates. Leave the aquarium light off for a few hours to give invertebrates a chance to acclimate.

Chapter 9

How and What to Feed Fish and Invertebrates

Feeding Fish

After good water quality, feeding is probably the next most important aspect in keeping fish healthy. There are an overwhelming number of different fish foods available including frozen, dry, freeze-dried and live foods. It is important to become acquainted with the types of food a fish requires before purchasing the fish (does it require high protein or extra vegetable matter?) It is best to feed frozen food as a staple and use dry foods to supplement. The key to keeping fish healthy and ensuring that they are getting a complete diet is to feed a variety of foods and/or add vitamins to the food.

Frozen Foods

There are countless frozen fish foods on the market today including specialty foods for particular species, foods that are blended for herbivores, carnivores, and omnivores. They are designed to copy the diversity of food that fish would get in the wild. Most blended foods consist primarily of various seafood and algae. Some manufacturers add color enhancers and vitamins. Blended foods are ideal for everyday feeding.

Prepared frozen fish food in easy pop-out cubes for carnivores, omnivores and herbivores

Specialty foods include krill, mysis shrimp, squid, mussels and plankton, to name a few. Your fish are the best indicators of what foods they like and do not like. It is best to use a wide variety to ensure a balanced and nutritious diet.

Frozen foods, stored properly, are about as close to fresh food as you can get. Some manufacturers use a gel binder to keep the food from falling apart once it defrosts. Other foods immediately begin to fall apart as they hit the water. Foods without a gel binder work well for smaller fish because they fall apart; larger fish prefer larger chunks and a gel binder will help keep the food together to keep them happy.

TIP: Thaw frozen food in RO/DI water to remove phosphates and other possible preservatives. Then, pour defrosted food through a fine fish net before feeding it to your fish. A few frozen food manufacturers rinse their foods prior to mixing and freezing. Some of these pre-rinsed foods have microparticles to feed corals and should not be rinsed again or fine particles will be removed.

Dry Foods

There have been many advances in dry foods to increase the nutritional value and keep vitamins from oxidizing. Remember, variety is the spice of life. While frozen is best as a main staple food, there are many excellent dry foods that can be added as supplements to increase the nutritional value of their diets. Again, your fish will let you know what they like.

To keep dry foods fresh, purchase small size containers. It is usually cheaper to buy bulk size containers of food but, from a freshness and nutritional standpoint, it is best to buy enough food to last 1 to 2 months.

Freeze Dried Foods

Freeze-dried foods are great supplements. The best feature about this type of food is its ability to soak up vitamins and trace elements - especially helpful when you have sick fish. Set the freeze-dried food of choice, such as freeze-dried krill, into a bowl and pour liquid fish vitamins over it. After a few minutes, the vitamins will soak into the food.

Algae Sheets

Many fish such as tangs, rabbit fish and most angels spend their days grazing the live rock looking for algae or seaweed. When an algae is in short supply or you want to supplement your fishes' diets, try algae sheets. These sheets are made of dried seaweed and are especially nutritious for fish. A product called a lettuce clip is available to hold the algae sheet in place via a suction cup or magnet. Place a sheet or strip of dried seaweed in the clip and attach the suction cup against the inside wall of the aquarium.

Seaweed and clip attached to front glass of aquarium

Feed algae strips daily if you have several herbivores and very little existing algae in your aquarium. Otherwise, feed a couple of times a week as a supplement. If the fish devour the algae sheet within the first few minutes, you can add all or part of another. The algae sheet will eventually decompose if not eaten.

> *TIP: If you have excess algae growing on your live rock, you may want to reduce the number of algae sheets you feed to force your herbivore(s) to graze naturally on the algae growing in the aquarium.*

Live Foods

Saltwater live foods such as brine shrimp (sea monkeys) and copepods (small crustaceans) will be quickly consumed by your fish. Copepods and brine shrimp are very small and are therefore perfect for small fish and finicky eaters.

Brine shrimp is often sold in too large a quantity to use in one feeding and you may need to set up a small holding tank to keep the excess. Copepods come in a bottle or container which can be used for storing. Depending on the type of copepod they may need to be refrigerated; some may be kept at room temperature.

Copepods can also be added to a refugium to establish a colony. Some copepods will be sucked up by the return water pump and wind up as food for your fish, invertebrates and corals. Others, hopefully, will remain in the refugium, grow and reproduce. Once a colony is established, use a fine mesh fish net to catch some of the larger copepods and feed to your fish.

Suggestions for Fussy Eaters

Some fish are finicky eaters or do not recognize food and must be enticed into eating something different from what they found in the wild. Try different types of foods; or add an appetite stimulator to encourage fish to eat. Many fish are used to eating live foods; you may want to try live brine shrimp and copepods.

Feeding Eels

Some eels are aggressive eaters while others sense food but are slow on the uptake to begin searching for it. If there are several aggressive eaters in an aquarium, it may difficult to get food to slower fish. For example, fish such as groupers and triggers are fast moving and aggressive eaters; they compete for large chunks towards the surface of the aquarium. Eels like snowflakes or morays often hide and will not generally swim to the surface to grab food. You may need to use a tool like long tongs to hold some food in front of the eel. Another option is to use a clear one-inch diameter tube (such as those used with undergravel filters) which is available in 3-foot sections. Just set one end of the tube into the aquarium, strategically near the eel. Drop chunks of fish food into the other end of the tube and viola! The food is safe from stout, intimidating tank mates and exits the tube directly in front of the eel. Make sure you feed the energetic eaters in the aquarium first; they should be full before you attempt to feed a restrained or passive eel.

Feeding Made Simple

It seems like feeding fish would be simple, but sometimes it takes a little forethought to make certain everyone gets a fair chance at the food. The real trick to successful feeding is to feed each fish well without over feeding the aquarium. You can accomplish this by paying close attention to the fish while you drop food into the water. Add a small amount of food and watch; if the fish eat it all, add more. Food should be consumed before hitting the bottom of the aquarium unless you are aiming to feed crabs or shrimp. If any food is left uneaten, remove it and feed less next time.

Try to feed fish around the same time every day. It is better to give your fish small amounts several times throughout the day rather than a large amount once a day. If there is extra food after fish have stopped eating, net it out or use a siphon to remove it. Thaw frozen food before feeding. Food that is prepared in a gelatinous base can be mashed into pieces for smaller fish after it is thawed.

Vitamins and Trace Elements

For vitamins to have the most effect, add them directly to the food instead of indirectly to the water. It may not be necessary to supplement with vitamins if your fish have a varied diet. However, since most fish eat a huge variety of food native to the area in which they are found, it is a good idea to add supplemental vitamins. Fish are the best indicator of their diet. If their colors are not vivid, adding vitamins to the food daily or several times a week can help.

Add liquid vitamins to frozen foods and soak the food as it thaws. As mentioned earlier, freeze-dried foods soak up vitamins and trace elements well. Set your freeze-dried food in a bowl and pour on the vitamins. After a few minutes, the vitamins are soaked into the food and most fish will eagerly consume this food.

Live brine shrimp can also soak up vitamins making a healthy treat for your fish. Fill a small bag about a quarter of the way with saltwater with a low salinity (around 1.008). Add 5-10 drops of your favorite vitamin supplement. Shake the bag well and add live brine. Let the shrimp sit for half an hour or so, strain them through a net and feed them to your fish.

Feeding While You Are On Vacation

Here are two good ways to keep your fish fed and your aquarium healthy while you are away.

First, use an automatic fish feeder that will feed your fish multiple times during the day. The feeder will dispense dry foods, both flakes and pellets.

On the other hand, if any of your fish will not consume dry food, create pre-measured food packets for your fish sitter. Separate frozen foods into single-serving containers or plastic bags so that a prearranged amount of food is available for each feeding.

Use the system mentioned earlier to keep your aquarium topped off by a fish sitter. Calculate how much water evaporates during a normal day. Have your fish sitter fill a container to the daily evaporation level (mark your container) with RO water or whichever water you normally use. Have them add the frozen food to the water to thaw. Since you are generally adding only a small amount of water it may not be necessary to remove chlorine, however, it will not hurt to use a few drops of a de-chlorinator. Once the food thaws, the fish sitter can simply pour the food and water slowly into the aquarium. Now, not only did the fish sitter feed the fish, but the aquarium is also topped off.

Feeding Invertebrates

In a reef aquarium most **crabs, shrimp and snails** are added as part of a cleanup crew. These foragers generally find plenty of food to eat. If they require additional food or you have non-cleanup animals go to "Invertebrates are Beneficial and Fun", Chapter 8, to find individual species recommendations.

Anemones have symbiotic algae (zooxanthellae) living in their tissue which, through photosynthesis, create nutrients. They will eat silversides (small whole fish) and chopped raw seafood like squid, krill, shrimp and fish.

Feather Dusters and Coco Worms eat phytoplankton, fine detritus from the water, oyster eggs, prepared liquid and frozen foods designed and labeled specifically for filter feeders. A turkey baster may be used to lightly blow food into the current towards the crown. If you try to blow food directly at the crown it will retract into its tube and will not eat.

Small to medium-size Brittle Stars and Serpent Stars are carnivores, making them excellent scavengers of detritus and uneaten meaty fish food.

Sand Sifting Sea Stars are omnivores. They eat detritus, small crustacean, microfauna (microscopic animals) and uneaten foods. In cleaner aquariums their diet can be supplemented with a small amount of fish food such as mysis shrimp. Feed them at night when the fish are resting.

Most **Sea Urchins** are great at eating many types of algae in a reef including coralline algae. They will also eat Nori seaweed, foods high in spirulina, kelp and other forms of algae.

Overfeeding

Overfeeding can cause water quality problems! In addition, uneaten, decaying food becomes food for unwanted algae such as filamentous and red slime algae (Cyanobacteria).

If an aquarium has been overfed and you are concerned, test the water for ammonia. Test the water the day of and day after the incident. Excess food can be siphoned out of the aquarium (explained in "How to Care for Your Aquarium", Chapter 11) and fresh saltwater replenished. If the ammonia level is high, do a significant water change of at least 25%. Test the levels later that day or the next day. The ammonia levels on an established aquarium will generally go back to zero within a short period of time.

Chapter 10

Setting Up a Saltwater Quarantine Tank

It is always a good idea to quarantine newly purchased saltwater fish rather than adding them directly from the store to an established aquarium. Many hobbyists skip this process, and some get lucky, but you should quarantine all new fish for at least three weeks before transferring them to their display aquarium. Most pet and aquarium stores do not have the space or time to quarantine fish.

FREE BONUS: Claim your FREE copy of "How You Can Select Healthy Fish, Like the Experts" at http://9nl.be/Freebonuses

Since the majority of saltwater fish are collected from the ocean, they endure a tremendous amount of stress while being snatched from their familiar surroundings, packed in plastic bags, stuffed in dark boxes and flown halfway around the world. They need time to recuperate, heal and get used to aquarium living.

The larger problem is if a sick fish goes into your reef it can infect your existing fish. What makes it worse it is very difficult to catch even a sick fish out of a reef packed with lots of rockwork. Save yourself some stress and quarantine all new fish.

Benefits of a Quarantine Aquarium

A quarantine aquarium, usually smaller than the show aquarium, is a place to acclimate new fish. Use it as a treatment or hospital aquarium for sick fish, a holding tank for aggressive fish, and even a recovery place for injured fish. Many of the supplies needed for this aquarium are similar to those needed for your show aquarium. Following is a list of equipment to build a quarantine tank along with necessary test kits.

Supplies and Equipment Needed
- 10 to 29 gallon aquarium - to keep fish up to five inches
- Filter - sponge filter or hang-on filter
- Submersible heater
- Thermometer
- Top - glass or plastic
- Light
- Plastic decorations or PVC pipe
- Hydrometer
- Net
- Siphon hose or gravel vacuum

Testing Supplies
- Hydrometer
- High range pH test kit
- Ammonia test kit
- Nitrite test kit
- Copper test kit

Eight Steps to Setting Up a Quarantine Tank

1. Rinse the aquarium with water only. If you have used this aquarium before, consider sterilizing it; use a light bleach solution as described later.

2. Place the aquarium on a stand or solid flat surface that can support its weight.

3. Attach a filter. Use a sponge filter or, preferably, a hang-on filter. Replace any cartridges with filter floss or a filter pad when medicating. Activated carbon found inside factory cartridges will remove most medications.

4. Attach a heater to the inside back of the aquarium, on the side opposite from the filter. Set the temperature between 78 and 80 degrees Fahrenheit.

5. Fill the aquarium with premix RO or RO/DI water. The water in the quarantine tank should have the same specific gravity and pH parameters as in your display aquarium. The temperature may be a little warmer than the show aquarium, though, as this will help speed up parasite cycles and/or diseases if you are treating fish.

6. Once the aquarium is full of water, turn on the filter. After about ten minutes, plug in the heater.

7. Place artificial plastic decorations throughout the aquarium.

8. Place a top and light on the aquarium. If possible, let the quarantine aquarium run for 24 hours to ensure the heater and filter are working properly. Otherwise, keep a close eye on the temperature and water movement.

Quarantine aquarium: filter, heater, light and decoration

Decorating a Quarantine Aquarium

Decorations in quarantine are very important. Decorations in a quarantine aquarium are not for our aesthetic enjoyment but they are there to provide fish with places to hide from us, to feel more secure and, overall, to have a quicker and healthier acclimation. Make sure there are enough hiding spots for all fish. Larger fish will naturally need larger decorations to feel comfortable.

Decorations should be plastic: PVC pipes, elbows or tees large enough for the fish to swim inside of are perfect; molded decorations are also fine. Many new hobbyists errantly use dead coral skeletons and shells to make the fish feel at home since those are things found in its natural habitat. **DO NOT use them**.

Sand or gravel is also not recommended for a quarantine aquarium. Dead coral skeletons, shells, crushed coral and aragonite (substrates) absorb copper and may absorb medications. Using coral of any size, or aragonite in a quarantine tank increases the amount of medication needed to dose the aquarium and/or the frequency that dosing is required. In addition, since a quarantine tank sometimes doubles as a treatment or "hospital" tank, it is a good idea to streamline what you use so that the décor can be used for either.

Add plastic or silk plants to finish create a safe-feeling habitat for your new fish.

Biological Filtration

Hospital or quarantine aquariums cycle like any other aquarium when they are first set up. Because these tanks are for new or sick fish, it is important to keep ammonia and nitrite levels in check so as not to further traumatize the already stressed fish.

One option is to keep a quarantine or hospital aquarium running all the time with some small or inexpensive fish in it. Another option is to keep a sponge or other easily removed media in your display aquarium sump on which to grow beneficial bacteria. This media is then ready to use in your hospital aquarium at a moment's notice. When you set up a quarantine aquarium, add the colonized media to the filter to help keep ammonia and nitrite levels from rising to toxic levels.

NOTE: Many antibiotics kill beneficial bacteria. Should fish require treatment with antibiotics it may be best to save the colonized media for another time.

If you must treat your fish with antibiotics, or if you do not have or simply choose not to use colonized media, be sure to closely monitor ammonia and nitrite levels and change water as often as is needed to keep them low or nonexistent. Test water daily, change water often, and you can still be successful.

Adding Fish

Take a few minutes to set a mood for moving fish. Turn off the aquarium light and dim the room lights. Make sure to acclimate (following acclimation methods in "Bringing Your New Fish Home" in Chapter 7) fish before releasing them into the quarantine aquarium. The size of the aquarium determines how many fish it can house together. Once you release the fish, let them relax for the first few hours or overnight before turning on the light. Turn the light on during the day and off at night. Turning the light on and off at the same time each day is another way to ease stress on tank inhabitants (use an appliance timer).

Feed fish a variety of foods lightly, twice a day. As always, feed only what your fish will eat without any food landing on the bottom of the aquarium. If you happen to overfeed, net or siphon out any extra food immediately.

Vitamins

Adding vitamins to fish food is a good idea to aid ailing fish and boost the immune systems of healthy fish.

Medications

Medications are a choice. You may wait and observe fish for any stressful signs without adding medications or you may add medication immediately. In any case, to strengthen the immune systems of fish, make sure water quality remains consistent.

Watching Ammonia and Nitrite Levels

Test water daily. The main levels of concern are ammonia and nitrite; these levels should remain at zero or very close to zero. Change water if they rise. Generally you would remove 25% to 50% of the water in the tank and refill it with clean saltwater of the same salinity, temperature and pH.

With the many different sized aquariums that can be used, the differing numbers and sizes of fish kept as well as varying feeding amounts, there are no hard, fast rules on how often to change water in a quarantine or hospital aquarium. The best indicator is to test water and watch the fish for signs of stress. Perform water changes with a gravel siphon (vacuum) or a section of 5/8" to 3/4" flexible tubing. Make sure you siphon any waste from the bottom of the aquarium.

Specific Gravity and pH Tests

Another level to watch is specific gravity. When water evaporates, pour only fresh RO water back into the aquarium. During water changes make sure specific gravity and temperature are constant. The final test is pH; make sure it reads between 8.1 and 8.3. If pH dips below 8.1, add a buffer to raise it slowly back up. Other tests may be required depending on use of medications. Unless the tank has been set up for a long time, there should be little reason to worry about nitrate levels.

When to Move Quarantine Fish to the Display Aquarium

If after three weeks a fish eats well and appears to be healthy, it is ready to move to your display aquarium. Follow the procedure to acclimate fish (see "Bringing Your New Fish Home" in Chapter 7).

Before you move the new fish, feed the fish in your display aquarium. Also, turn the light off for a few hours to calm tank inhabitants and help keep them from harassing new arrivals.

Medicating Sick or Wounded Fish

Try never to put medications into your reef aquarium.

If the aquarium is not already set up, fill the hospital tank halfway with water from your display aquarium and the rest with mixed saltwater of the same salinity, temperature and pH to make the transfer less stressful on the patient.

If the aquarium is already set up, acclimate the fish by either using the drip method or by floating them in a bag and adding water slowly over time.

If a fish has torn fins, it will generally heal on its own; if there are wounds on the side of its body, it may be necessary to treat the water to keep any infections at bay.

When treating sick fish, a hospital tank is the best place to do it. As mentioned before, water quality has to be very good for these fish to get better. The key to healing sick and stressed fish is to get their immune systems up to speed and let the fish cure themselves.

Chapter 11

How to Care for Your Aquarium

As with all living things, it takes routine maintenance to keep fish healthy and an aquarium looking great. The best way to avoid stress and, ultimately, diseases is to keep the water in the aquarium in ideal condition entails regular water changes, siphoning (vacuuming) the substrate and cleaning equipment. Not everything has to be done at once, though.

Here is a breakdown of things to do and how often we need to do them.

Daily

Not all maintenance has to do with getting your hands wet. Some of it is just plain fun! Feed your fish at least once each day (Detailed feeding information in "How and What to Feed Fish and Invertebrates", Chapter 9.) Take a few minutes to observe your fish and watch them eat. Make sure they are all able to get food and learn their habits, so that you will be able to recognize what is **normal** for each fish. Check for clamped fins, white spots, labored breathing, abnormal hiding, etc. Also feed corals regularly and observe their health and eating habits.

Check the temperature and make sure it is between 76° and 78°. Salt never evaporates, so add salt-free RO or RO/DI (de-chlorinated municipal) water to your aquarium when the water level drops. Check to make sure your filter and pumps are working properly. Make certain that water is physically moving in your aquarium.

If the water is cloudy or smells bad test the ammonia and nitrite levels. Cloudy water could indicate that the fish have been overfed (it only takes overfeeding once to foul the water); it could also indicate that one (or more) of your fish is dead and decaying. If anything looks amiss, is it prudent to find the underlying reason so you can correct it.

Weekly

Algae is natural and overall helpful in an aquarium, but it is difficult to see through when it grows on the glass. Using an algae magnet (so you don't get your hands wet) clean the algae from the sides of the aquarium as it grows. It just takes a minute or two if you keep up with it regularly. Empty and clean the protein skimmer waste collection cup and rinse or change the mechanical filter media. (Mechanical filter media include socks, pads, and cartridges.)

Biweekly / Monthly

Some aquariums require small biweekly water changes; others are good for once a month. Either way, water changes require some time. You will want to siphon or vacuum debris from the substrate and clean the filter and other equipment.

Every 6 to 12 Months

Replace Light Bulbs

In a reef aquarium, fluorescent, compact fluorescent and metal halide bulbs should be replaced every 6 to 12 months depending on the lamp and ballast. Animals such as sea anemones and corals use light as a food source, so to keep these animals healthy change bulbs when recommended.

Replace UV Sterilizer Bulbs

UV sterilizer bulbs should be replaced every 6 to 12 months depending on the ballast. Over time, a UV bulb loses its intensity; it becomes ineffective in killing parasites, bacteria, fungi and algae.

Some convenient items to have on hand when preparing to clean your aquarium

Here is a list of some of the most pertinent equipment you will need in order to change water in and clean your aquarium:

Water change supplies
- Gravel vacuum (siphon)
- Algae scraper
- Algae magnet or sponge
- Salt mix
- Hydrometer
- Thermometer
- Water conditioner
- Aquarium glass cleaner
- Towels
- Fish net
- Turkey baster (used to blow debris off live rock)
- Clean bucket (used only for water changes)

Testing supplies
- Hydrometer
- pH test kit
- Ammonia test kit
- Nitrite test kit
- Nitrate test kit
- Carbonate hardness test kit
- Optional test kits - phosphates, copper

15 Steps to Maintaining a Saltwater Aquarium

Step 1: Inspect Fish Health

Watch your fish. If they are ordinarily out and swimming around and are now hiding there could be a problem. Make sure their eyes are clear, they are not breathing heavily and the body and fins are clear of any abnormalities such as tears or chunks missing. For close inspection, use a magnifying glass.

Step 2: Test the Water

- Use aquarium test kits to test ammonia, nitrite, nitrate, carbonate hardness.
- Ammonia and nitrite should read zero.
- For the health of your fish keep nitrates below 50 mg/L, for invertebrates and coral this level should be much lower, not to exceed 10 mg/L. Frequent, consistent water changes are the best solution to keep nitrates in check.
- Keep pH between 8.2 and 8.4.
- Carbonate hardness or alkalinity should be between 8 to 11dkh.
- Use a hydrometer to test specific gravity or salinity. Specific gravity should be between 1.020 and 1.025.
- Check the aquarium temperature and ensure it is between 76° and 78° year round.

Step 3: Clean Algae from Interior Glass

Clean or scrape algae off the inside walls of the aquarium with a hand held algae pad, a pad on a stick or an algae magnet. As you move the outside magnet around, the inside magnet scrapes off algae. Standard algae magnets are good for soft algae but hard algae or coralline may require a scraper with a metal blade. A razor blade scraper may be used on glass aquariums, but be careful around silicone seals. Acrylic aquariums call for special tools to keep from scratching the surface.

Step 4: Clean Decorations and Live Rock

If you are using artificial decorations and they need cleaning, remove them from the aquarium to clean them. Normally there is no need to scrub live rock clean. Fish and invertebrates like to graze the rocks for algae. Over time detritus and debris builds up on the rock. Use a turkey baster to blast water at the rocks blowing off the detritus and debris to the bottom of aquarium. You can also use a six to eight foot piece of flexible tubing 1/2" to 5/8" in diameter to siphon detritus from live rocks into a bucket. If you really want to scrub the live rock, use a small brush or toothbrush.

Step 5: Unplug Equipment

During the water change it is necessary to unplug or turn off the electrical equipment. Unplug or turn off the power strips that the protein skimmer water pump(s), return water pump and heater are plugged into. If the powerheads are attached close to the surface of the aquarium they will also need to be unplugged. Unplug everything except perhaps some light so that you can see what you are doing. To make servicing the aquarium easier, put all the equipment that needs to be unplugged on the same electrical power strip. This way you can quickly turn off the power and easily turn the power back on when you are finished.

Step 6: Vacuum Substrate and Remove Water

It is now time to clean the substrate. Place the large end of the gravel vacuum into the aquarium and the long flexible tube end into a bucket. Start the siphon by following the manufacturer's directions. The water should now be flowing into the bucket. Push the gravel vacuum into the sand to remove accumulated detritus and water at the same time. Try to vacuum as much of the substrate as possible. If water flows too quickly, pinch the flexible tubing to slow the water flow. Keep an eye on how much water you are removing. You can complete small water changes of 10 to 15% every other week, or change at least 25% once per month. If you have sand-sifting starfish or other invertebrates in the sand, take care not to injure them when vacuuming the substrate.

Step 7: Add Saltwater, Test and Add Additives

Using a hydrometer, test the specific gravity of your aquarium water. It should read between 1.020 and 1.025. If it reads too high, decrease it by adding less salt to the replacement water. If the salinity reads too low, simply mix replacement water to a slightly higher salinity. For example, if your aquarium water has specific gravity of 1.027, add replacement saltwater with a specific gravity of 1.022.

If you are using premixed saltwater you bought from a store to fill your aquarium then follow the premixed saltwater section directions. If you need to mix your own RO or RO/DI saltwater then go to the section below labeled mixing your own saltwater.

Premixed Saltwater

If you are using premix RO or RO/DI saltwater you purchased from the store it is still a good idea to run a few tests. Test the specific gravity, it should read between 1.020 and 1.025. If the specific gravity is too low, add more salt. If you add too much salt and the hydrometer reads over the target, remove some of the water and add fresh RO water.

Test pH and make sure it is between 8.2 and 8.4. If the pH is below 8.2, add a buffering agent to adjust it (Information about pH can be found in "Water Quality Explained", Chapter 6.) The water should be around room temperature, though that may be a few degrees cooler then the aquarium. Since we are changing a small amount of water, the difference in temperature should not make a huge difference and will not make a significant change in the aquarium's water temperature. If the water is very cold, let it adjust to room temperature before beginning a water change.

Mixing Your Own Saltwater

If you have your own RO filter system or use municipal water, begin by filling a 5-gallon bucket or larger non-toxic container (preferably with wheels) with water. Next, add salt to the water. Follow the instructions on the salt mix, keeping in mind that a general rule is to add approximately one cup of salt to every two gallons of aquarium water.

After thoroughly mixing salt with the water in the bucket, use a hydrometer to test specific gravity.

Mixing and testing saltwater levels with a hydrometer

The specific gravity should read between 1.020 and 1.025. If the specific gravity is too low, add more salt. If you add too much salt and the hydrometer reads over the target, remove some of the water and add fresh RO or de-chlorinate water.

The RO filter system should have removed chlorine and/or chloramines; therefore a water conditioner is not necessary. Test pH and make sure it is between 8.2 and 8.4. If the pH is below 8.2, add a buffering agent to adjust it (Information about pH can be found in "Water Quality Explained", Chapter 6.)

Step 8: Adding Saltwater Back to the Aquarium

If using artificial decorations use a second set of clean ones to redecorate the aquarium. To replace water, just pour the premixed saltwater directly from the bucket or container into the aquarium; or use a water pump to return water to the aquarium. A submersible water pump attached to a six-foot piece of flexible tubing is useful when changing large amounts of water. Pumping the water into the aquarium takes less muscle. If you are using a bucket, you will need to pour the water slowly onto one of the live rocks close to the water level or into the aquarium water. Fill an undrilled aquarium until the water level is above the bottom of the aquarium's frame.

Drilled aquariums fill until water begins to flow over the overflow. At this point you can either continue to add water to the aquarium to fill the Berlin sump in the cabinet or you can pour water directly into the sump until filled to the designated max fill line.

If sand is blown onto rocks or corals use a turkey baster to squirt it to the bottom of the aquarium.

Step 9: Clean or Change Filter Media

Clean all mechanical filter media, including foam, pads, filter socks and cartridges often, and replace them as needed. To clean mechanical media rinse it under running water until water runs through it clear (foam and some pads can be squeezed or wrung out). If the mechanical filter is your main source of biological filtration, clean the filter in de-chlorinated water. Most tap water contains chlorine or chloramines that will kill beneficial bacteria.

If using filter socks, keep extra ones on hand to replace dirty ones. To clean filter socks put them in a washing machine **by themselves**. Add a quarter cup (less if using a high efficiency washer) of bleach (no additives) to your detergent compartment. Do not use detergent! Once the washing cycle is complete, run the socks through a second rinse cycle with no bleach, just water. Remove socks and let them air dry.

> *TIP: The more often you clean or replace filter media, the better the water quality of the aquarium. A dirty mechanical filter will eventually lead to increased nitrates as bacteria begin to grow in the media to process the excess waste. It is important to clean and/or replace the physical filter media often.*

Replace carbon each month. While it may last longer than a month, it may not, and its life depends on how heavily a reef is stocked. There are many different types of resins that are also helpful in a reef aquarium; if you use any of these, change them according to manufacturer's recommendations.

Step 10: Harvest Algae

When using a refugium to help absorb excess nutrients, harvest part of the macro algae whenever it becomes dense. Trim, thin and remove some macro algae when the compartment is full. If you like, you can change a small amount of water in the refugium to remove detritus from the top of the substrate only. Removing excess algae creates room for more nutrient needing algae to grow and remove excess nutrients from your reef.

> *CAUTION: Never disturb the sand bed in a refugium. Because there is little or no oxygen in the sand bed, it is a great place for hydrogen sulfide to hide. Disturbing this bed will release this harmful chemical into your aquarium, potentially killing your livestock!*

Also the side of the refugium may get covered in micro algae or coraline algae and need to be scraped. The scraping of coraline algae is to view inside the filter therefore all sides do not have to be scraped.

Step 11: Cleaning the Protein Skimmer and Other Equipment

Dump and clean any skimmate (waste) collected in the protein skimmer cup. This waste is usually extremely foul smelling. Clean the collection cup and throat with a bottlebrush. Protein skimmers should be completely taken apart and cleaned every four to six months. For protein skimmers with venturi, clean the venturi regularly to keep salt from building up and reducing airflow.

If using a UV sterilizer, check to be certain the bulb is burning. UV bulbs should be replaced according to the manufacturer suggestions, usually every six to twelve months.

Powerheads can be quickly taken apart and cleaned with a small brush every one to three months.

Canister or hang-on filters should be taken apart and cleaned regularly to ensure good water flow.

Step 12: Clean the Exterior Glass

Clean outside glass on aquarium with plain water or an aquarium glass cleaner and a soft rag or paper towel.

Step 13: Clean Inside and Outside the Stand

Wipe down inside and outside of the cabinet or stand. Salt creep buildup can be wiped off with a damp towel or can be vacuumed with a shop vac. **Excess salt creep around hoses and PVC parts may indicate a fitting that needs attention.**

Step 14: Keep a Log or Diary

Keeping a diary or a log is useful for keeping track of water changes. The more consistent you are with water changes, the better the water quality will be for your fish. Filling out a log regularly and recording water tests can also ensure water parameters stay at acceptable levels.

Tracking sheets are handy to keep water changes on track

Livestock Log - This sheet tracks your livestock purchases. When you shop for new fish, corals or invertebrates, take this log with you to ensure your new animal will be compatible with the ones you already have. You can track costs, but the greatest advantage to tracking is so that you can take pride in keeping your fish, corals and invertebrates healthy for years and knowing their ages. Other log sheets keep track of water changes and aquarium parameters such as ammonia, pH and other levels.

DOWNLOAD YOUR FREE BONUSES: Livestock, Water Testing and Medication Tracking Sheets at http://9nl.be/Freebonuses

Step 15: Clean Light Bulbs and Fixtures

If light bulbs are exposed to salt water, salt will accumulate on them, cutting down their efficiency. To clean fluorescent and power compact bulbs turn them off and unplug them. Let them cool down and it is best to remove the bulbs from their fixture. Mix freshwater with a little vinegar or rubbing alcohol; use either solution on a damp soft cloth. Gently clean bulbs with the vinegar/water mixture or alcohol and gently wipe the salt off the bulbs (metal halide manufactures recommend not to touch the bulbs with your hands). Dry the bulbs and return them to the fixture. If the salt does not come off or is caked on, consider replacing the bulb. If you choose to clean the bulbs while they remain in the fixture above the aquarium, make sure large chunks of salt do not fall onto sea anemones or live corals. Also, if you have a glass or plastic shield protecting the bulbs, keeping it clean will allow a brighter aquarium. Use the same mixture as mentioned above to clean its shield. A razor blade may be necessary to scrape buildup off glass.

Now it is YOUR turn!

Armed with the information you have learned in this guide, you now have a firm foundation and understanding of how to assemble, stock, and care for your own saltwater aquarium.

You are about to start an amazing adventure by creating your own underwater masterpiece.

Find other books and products by Laurren Schmoyer at http://Aquatic Experts.com.

CLAIM YOUR FREE GIFTS: Thank you for purchasing this saltwater guide. To download your Special FREE Bonuses including useful tracking forms, My Perfect Fish Identifier Form, and more, go to http://9nl.be/Freebonuses

More Books by the Author on Amazon

There are few things more relaxing than watching a living reef aquarium filled with bright, exotic, colorful fish. Your eyes are soon transfixed on the breath-taking corals with their mind-blowing colors and endless shapes. Having your own living reef is the ultimate hobby and a spectacular achievement.

To create a thriving living reef takes the right equipment, knowledge, compatible livestock and routine care. Over 25 years of working with reefs Laurren Schmoyer has discovered many hidden secrets and has finally created a blue print to help you build your own amazing living reef aquarium! His book is packed with pictures to guide you through each step in creating, stocking and caring for your reef.

This book shows a step-by-step process for assembling a reef aquarium. Follow these steps to expertly set up your reef.

There are hundreds of species of beautiful saltwater fish available to hobbyists. But, how do you know which are safe to add to a reef aquarium? Fortunately, you do not have to harm any fish or waste your money purchasing fish that are not compatible in reef aquariums. In this book you will find lists of brightly-colored fish which are safe to use.

The addition of live corals can transform an ordinary saltwater fish aquarium into a beautiful, vibrant underwater world. Corals are available in nearly every color imaginable and in a huge variety of shapes and sizes. Some sway with water currents while others tower majestically in brilliant blues, purples, reds and greens. The fact is, some corals are very aggressive and will attack other corals. Choosing compatible corals takes knowledge which this book delivers.

Mixing corals, invertebrates and fish from all over the world is both a skill and an art. This book will give YOU the confidence and knowledge to create your own underwater masterpiece. If you're serious about wanting to create your own gorgeous, living slice of the ocean, then you need to order a copy of *The New Reef Aquarium: Setup, Care and Compatibility* right now!

Aquatic Experts Series

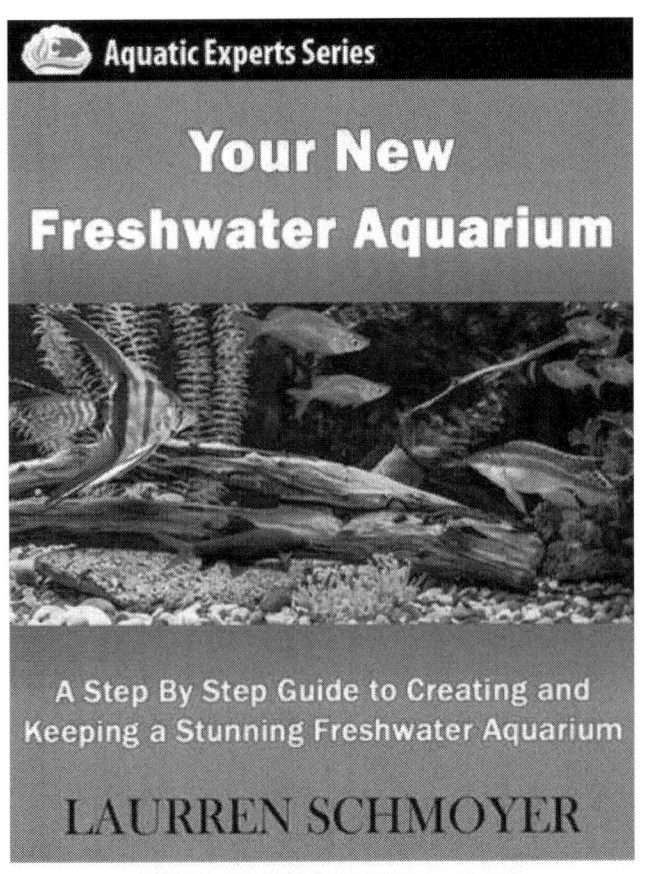

Your New Freshwater Aquarium

A Step By Step Guide to Creating and Keeping a Stunning Freshwater Aquarium

LAURREN SCHMOYER

[Buy from amazon.com]

Have you ever dreamed of owning a beautiful, crystal clear freshwater aquarium filled with schools of lively, graceful fish, with gentle bubbles flowing peacefully behind them? How about enjoying it all with very little care?

You can use Laurren's foolproof, straightforward, easy-to-understand blueprint for setting up, keeping and maintaining your own beautiful aquarium. It is called *Your New Freshwater Aquarium: A Step by Step Guide to Creating and Keeping a Stunning Freshwater Aquarium* and It ensures a perfect environment to keep your fish healthy and thriving.

In this guide you will learn about the equipment necessary to setup your aquarium; it also includes professional advice on the three types of filtration you must have for your aquarium to thrive. This guide will help take the guess-work out of stocking your new aquarium with examples of fully-stocked aquariums containing hardy, compatible colorful fish for various size aquariums. The guide explains how many fish to add when you first set up your aquarium, when to add more and even what fish can make up a well-stocked aquarium.

You will learn the most efficient way to care for and maintain your aquarium. These are exact techniques and instructions that my professional service technicians use. There are more - tons more -of expert tips throughout the guide.

If you want to create your own beautiful relaxing aquarium stocked with schools of colorful fish and a gentle stream of air bubbles, then you need to order your own copy of *Your New Freshwater Aquarium: A Step by Step Guide to Creating and Keeping a Stunning Freshwater Aquarium* right now!

Appendix

How to Cure Rock Taken From the Ocean

Live rock is used to create reef-like structures in both saltwater fish and reef aquariums. Since the rock is collected directly from oceans around the world it is inhabited with algae, animals, plants, bacteria and more. When it is shipped, some of the animal and plant life on the rock are damaged. These rocks must be cured or cleaned before they are safe to put with fish and invertebrates.

The rock arrives in a Styrofoam box and is usually wrapped in wet newspaper to keep it moist. Prepare a bucket of premixed saltwater to a specific gravity between 1.020 and 1.024.

1. Remove the rock from the box carefully. If you wish, wear rubber gloves. Look for any bristleworms that may be hanging partially out of the rock. These worms can sting or bite so use tweezers to remove them.

2. Dip the rock into the bucket of premixed dechlorinated salt water to remove any loose debris. Look for any white, slimy areas or decaying areas. Any decay should be removed with a brush. If you choose to do so, you may remove the algae and plant growth.

3. The rock can be placed into your aquarium or into a holding container while the rock cycles. If you choose to place it in an aquarium no animals may be added until the levels of ammonia and nitrite have dropped back to zero. This can take from 3 to 6 weeks.

4. When placing live rock in an aquarium try to keep as much of the rock off the bottom of the aquarium as possible to ensure good water circulation around the rock. As you build rock walls and cliffs you want as little contact between each piece of rock as possible. This again allows for good circulation and will create great hiding places for the fish.

5. Use powerheads, water pumps and the return pump outlets to direct water flow throughout the rock structure.

6. Make sure your protein skimmer is running properly. It should produce a thick, dark-colored waste in the collection cup. Activated

filter carbon may be used to remove organic waste and the smell. Set the heater between 76° and 78°.

7. The levels of nutrients in the water will begin to rise very rapidly. Keep the aquarium light off. If you keep a light on the aquarium it will grow a lot of unwanted algae.

8. Water changes should be done regularly. While removing the water use a piece of flexible tubing and siphon the white spots or any other dying debris off your rocks when they appear. Also siphon the bottom of the aquarium or container removing any debris. Change at least 50%, up to 100% of the water each time you do a water change. The more often the water changes are done, the lower the waste levels will be and the more plants and animals will survive.

9. When the levels of ammonia and nitrite read zero on your test kit the rock is cycled. Now you can gradually increase the amount of light each day, as well as the amount of time it stays on.

If you have not done a water change recently do one before adding fish, corals or invertebrates.

It takes patience to cure live rock. When the cycle completes, your aquarium will come to life as you begin adding colorful, playful, eye-catching fish, corals and invertebrates!

Glossary

Algae - plant-like organisms that conduct photosynthesis like larger plants, but lack stems, roots and leaves.

Ammonia - (NH3) - Toxin formed when fish waste and organic matter decompose. Consumed by Nitrosomonas bacteria.

Aragonite - Is found in nature and makes a perfect substrate for saltwater aquariums. As the pH of an aquarium drops below 8.2, aragonite dissolves releasing calcium, trace elements and carbonate. Carbonate is a buffer that keeps your pH up.

Bacteria Starter - Products that contain live cultures of beneficial bacteria used to shorten the Cycle period.

Berlin Filter - an external tank housing the mechanical filtration of a drilled aquarium. Berlin filters often also contain protein skimmers and heaters.

De-chlorinator - Product that removes chlorine from water. Some de-chlorinators also remove ammonia and chloramines.

Filtration - Methods of cleaning/purifying aquarium water. Three major types:
- Mechanical: Physical trapping of suspended particles, accomplished by filter pads or foam.
- Chemical: Trapping of dissolved matter, accomplished with carbon and filter media.
- Biological: Breakdown of harmful compounds, accomplished by beneficial bacteria.

Gravel Vacuum - Siphon tube and hose, used to plunge into gravel to remove detritus.

Heater - Heating element housed in glass or shatter-resistant composite tube. Place the heater near the filter intake to distribute heat evenly.

Hydrometer - An instrument used to measure specific gravity.

Nitrate (NO3-) - End product of Nitrogen Cycle, and least harmful nitrogen compound. Used by plants as fertilizer.

Nitrite (NO2-) - Toxin formed from breakdown of ammonia. Consumed by Nitrospira bacteria.

Nitrogen Cycle - Natural process occurring in all living bodies of water - it is the breakdown of organic matter and waste products into ammonia, then nitrite, then nitrate.

Nitrosomonas - Beneficial bacteria that consume toxic ammonia.

Nitrospira - Beneficial bacteria that consumes toxic nitrite.

PAR Meter - A PAR (Photo-synthetically Active Radiation) meter measures the light in a reef to ensure the proper wavelengths for corals at particular depths in the aquarium. Once we know the PAR value, we have a better idea of what types of corals to select as well as general placement in a reef aquarium.

pH - Measure of how acidic or basic a solution is on a scale from 0-14. Numbers below seven indicate acid, seven is neutral, and numbers above seven indicate base.

Sessile Invertebrates - Invertebrates which attach or anchor themselves in one place. Good examples are barnacles, corals and sponges.

Specific Gravity - The ratio of the mass of a solid or liquid to the mass of an equal volume of distilled water at 4°C (39°F). In a saltwater aquarium we measure specific gravity with a hydrometer and change it by adding either salt or water to get a reading of 1.020 to 1.025. This reading will change with temperature variations.

Sump - a holding tank that goes below an aquarium. It can be made of plastic, glass or acrylic. Water is routed from an aquarium down to fill the sump. Then a pump is placed in the sump to pump the water back to the aquarium. The sump holds equipment such as protein skimmer, heaters, etc.

Wet/Dry Filter - an external tank housing the mechanical and biological filtration of a drilled aquarium. Wet/dry filters often also contain protein skimmers and heaters.

More About the Author

Laurren Schmoyer at age 13 got his first job at a pet store. His love for animals prompted his study in Biology at University of North Carolina at Greensboro. After graduating from college, he searched for a career he could enjoy. Keeping fish aquariums both as a hobby and a job seemed like the ideal solution; Laurren opened an aquarium service company and began servicing aquariums in the Greensboro area. Immediately his phone started ringing with simple fish-keeping questions. Laurren felt the area needed a knowledgeable aquarium store. Armed with ambition, no money and a baby on the way he decided to create one. In a family-owned space, the tiny fish store materialized.

Since these meager beginnings, Aquamain's Fish World grew into one of the largest aquarium stores on the east coast. Laurren grew his small retail aquarium store of 1,500 square feet into a 10,000 square foot superstore. After 25 years, Laurren left Aquamain's Fish World, taking with him the aquarium service clients and opened a new aquarium service company to pursue a different adventure. He has spent many years teaching and training his customers in the experts' way to keep fish, plants, invertebrates and corals healthy and thriving for years. His desire and passion is to share his knowledge so that anyone can be a successful hobbyist. His products can be found at http://AquaticExperts.com.

Printed in Great Britain
by Amazon